SYMBOLS OF TRADE

SYMBOLS OF TRADE

Your Favorite Trademarks and the Companies They Represent

By Stanley Sacharow

ART DIRECTION BOOK COMPANY, NEW YORK

ISBN: 0-910158-98-3
Library of Congress Catalog Card No.: 82-073349

Printed in the United States of America.

Published by
Art Direction Book Company
10 East 39th Street
New York, New York 10016

For my sons, Scott Hunter and Brian Evan.

ACKNOWLEDGEMENT

For my wife, Beverly Lynn, whose research and help made this book possible. Her work in both the organization of material and her contribution of various chapters was enormous.

It has gotten to be that manufacturers with highly sophisticated technical help can almost immediately copy a competitor's product, stripping that competitor of the ability to promote an exclusive product benefit.

So, consumer benefits have become mere perceptions created by advertising. This is what has caused the great boom in the licensing business. Big money is being spent to use the names of actors, athletes, cartoon characters and even animals to give a product some apparent product difference in the marketplace.

Fruit of the Loom and Stetson, for example, do not make anything. They promote their name as a symbol of quality; and others pay a royalty to use the name.

New York Times (Jan. 7, 1982)

TABLE OF CONTENTS

LIST OF ILLUSTRATIONS

LIST OF TABLES

PREFACE

A social history of brand names is in many respects a history of industrialization, commerce and even of man himself. It is the story of how manufacturers attempted "to reach over the shoulder of the retailer, straight to the consumer."

As manufacturers began to see that containers and products demanded individuality, names and designs began to evolve out of the traditional subjects of the day. Tobacco appropriated the Indian, cleansers used a Black theme and laundry starch featured Chinese personalities on their package. Marks were also used to associate merchandise with great personalities of the day. There were Kossuth Oysters, Dewey Cigars and even Telephone Headache Tablets, after Dr. Alexander Graham Bell.

From these early beginnings came an increasing array of trademarks—often each with a story of its own to captivate the imagination of the consumer. In a sense, that is what this book is all about. It is a book about stories—stories behind famous trademarks and names—all intertwined in the framework of history and in the development of modern business.

Credit for producing a book must be given to many people and companies. This is the first book I have written with my wife, Beverly, as co-author. She has brought to the book a view that, hopefully, has given the work greater depth and understanding. I deeply appreciate her efforts and look forward toward producing many more works with her assistance.

Stanley Sacharow
East Brunswick, New Jersey

"In the foreground on a rock, with the word chemistry upon it is an eagle holding in his mouth a paintpot or cannister, with a brush, and a ribbon or streamer, on which are the words, Economical, Durable, Beautiful."

From the First Registered U.S. Trademark (Averill Paint Company, Oct. 25, 1870).

1

WHAT IT ALL MEANS

"With products, as with people—if there were no trademarks by which to identify articles of merchandise, there would be no way to tell the good from the bad."

Edward Rogers in *The Lanham Act and the Social Function of Trademarks* (1949)

Many people working in the graphic arts and advertising fields use the terms *brand*, *brandname*, *trademark* and *copyright* interchangeably. In many cases, this may be correct. But in still more situations legal restrictions and definitions have created distinct boundaries between each of these terms.

In the American Marketing Association's publication, "Marketing Definitions: A Glossary of Marketing Terms", *brand** is defined as "a name, term, symbol, or design, or a combination of them which is intended to identify the goods or services of one seller or group of sellers and to differentiate them from those of competitors." It is an all-inclusive term that in one way or another includes other, more particularized terms.

A *brand name* consists of words, letters and/or numbers which may be vocalized. On the other hand, a *tradename* relates to a business and is synonymous with the company name. A *brand mark* is the part of the brand which appears in the form of a symbol, color or design. A consumer recognizes the brand mark by sight and it is not expressed when she pronounces the brand. David Ogilvy calls the brand mark "a first class ticket through life" and issues one to each of his clients, deliberately designed to raise their social status. Mr. Clean, Del Monte and Arrow are brand names. California Packaging Corporation, Johnson and Johnson and The Quaker Oats Company are trade-

---

*The English word "brand" is derived from the Anglo-Saxon verb meaning "to burn." The word survives not only in its literal sense, but also in the expression "brand name."

names. The bear of Hamm's beer, Elsie, the Borden's cow and Planter's, "Mr. Peanut" are brand marks.

A *trademark* is defined by the American Marketing Association as a brand which has been given *legal protection* because under the law it has been appropriated exclusively by one seller. The modern trademark fits the definition in the Lanham Act*, "Any word, name, symbol, or device or any combination thereof adopted and used by a manufacturer or merchant to identify his goods and distinguish them from those manufactured or sold by others." Other marks can also be registered under the Trademark Act (see Table 1.1). All trademarks are brands and thus may include the words, letters or numbers which may be pronounced. They may also include a pictorial design (brand mark). It is wrong to consider the trademark as only the pictorial part of the brand.**

Copyright is legal protection the federal government gives the creator or owner of original wording, sounds or pictures presented as expressions. Materials that are copyrighted should carry in a prominent place a copyright notice: the word "copyright" and/or an abbreviation of the letter "C" in a circle, along with the name of the owner of the copyright and the year of

TABLE 1.1

OTHER MARKS CAPABLE OF REGISTRATION

Type of Mark	Definition	Example
Service Mark	A mark used in sales or advertising to identify the services of one person and distinguish them from the services of another.	Titles, character names, distinctive features of radio or TV programs i.e. *One Man's Family.*
Certification Mark	A mark used by one or more persons other than the owner of the mark to certify the regional origin, material, mode of manufacture, quality etc. of goods or services, or to certify that the work on these goods or services was performed by members of a union or organization.	*ILGWU*—Union Mark on Clothes, *Good Housekeeping Seal of Approval.*
Collective Mark	A mark used by members of a cooperative, association or other collective group, including unions.	*Shaker*—herbs, *Darigold*, used as a farm group to identify their dairy products.

*In effect since July 5, 1947.
**A particularly interesting work illustrating early 20th century U.S. trademarks is: Joseph Sinel, *A Book of American Trade-Marks and Devices* (Alfred A. Knopf), New York (1924).

copyright. Illustrations, devices and written matter appearing on packages come within the scope of copyright but, as in most cases, so much depends upon the degree of originality.

A greatly expanded and revised set of copyright laws went into effect on January 1, 1978. Very minimal changes had been made since 1909, and in the intervening 69 years many new methods of reproduction and communication had been developed. The new laws attempt to cover all of these. But perhaps most important is the change in the duration of copyright. Under the old law, the initial period of copyright was 28 years from the date on which copyright was secured, with the option of a single 28-year renewal, a total of 56 years. Under the new law, works in their renewal period before 1978 have the renewal time extended to 47 years, a total of 75 years. Works that have copyright renewed after 1978 also get a 47 year period of renewal. Copyrights initially secured in 1978 or after last until 50 years after the author's death. In the case of anonymous or pseudonymous works, or works on which the copyright is owned by an employer rather than by their creator, the duration is 75 years from publication or 100 years from creation, whichever period ends first.

BRANDS

A brand makes it easy for a consumer to identify a product or a service. It assures consumers that they are receiving comparable quality when they are reordering and getting a consistent product for their money. It is for this very reason that brand names sell better in poorer areas than do private labels or house brands. The poor person obtains both an "identity" with the product and a standard of integrity.*

Perhaps the ultimate reaction to a brand name was described in the *New Yorker* (1951),

> To a curly-headed four-year-old being tucked under the covers we posed this question: "Susie, which product brushes teeth whiter?" "Colgate's, of course, Gramp." We couldn't resist another. "Which product washes clothes cleaner?" Without a moment's hesitation: "Tide". We tried once more. "Which coffee gives the best value?" When she replied, "A and P, and now good-night, Gramp", we hurried out.

---

*A recent survey conducted by the National Consumer Institute (Mexico) showed that 85 percent of the children questioned recognized the trademark of a brand of potato chips but only 65 percent identified Mexico's national emblem. In another poll, only 14 percent recognized the Monument of Revolution in Mexico City, but 70 percent identified the symbol of a brand of cornflakes.

For the seller, a brand can be advertised and has a distinct recognition factor when displayed in a store. It tends to reduce price comparisons on two items with different brands. It also adds a measure of prestige to an otherwise ordinary product such as Domino sugar, Chiquita bananas and Morton salt.

THE NAME GAME

"The world is just running out of names. We have used computers to search through 128,000 words in order to produce one that is both appropriate and unclaimed."
Walter P. Margulies (1980)

Selecting a good brand name is often a difficult and unrewarding job. Back in 1909, Calkins and Holden wrote in *Modern Advertising*, "many names of widely advertised articles are grotesque, meaningless, hard to remember, uncouth, and in every way ill fitted to serve the purpose". It's hardly changed in over 70 years! In a study made several years ago, it was found that only 12 percent of the names helped sell the product; 36 percent actually hurt sales, and 52 percent were "nonentities"—contributing absolutely nothing to the sales appeal of the product" (see Table 1.2).

Think of the power of the symbolic value of a strong name, and all that it implies—Rolls-Royce, Hilton, Chanel, Lux. These are all symbols, and all are attitude-inducing and behavior-inducing, because they are intimately related to the values and norms of the society we live in.

Frequently the idea for a name and/or mark is suggested by one person and executed by several, or vice-versa. Many famous designers have spent major parts of their careers attempting to relieve the dull aesthetic level of most American trademarks. In past decades, designers such as W. A. Dwiggins, Harvey Hopkins Dunn, T. M. Cleland, C. B. Falls, Edward Penfield and Rene Clarke have all contributed their energies to this area. Particularly good

TABLE 1.2

DEVISING TRADEMARKS

Type	Example of Brand
Coined Word	Kodak, Exxon, Yuban, Uneeda, Häagen-Dazs, Charmin, Fresca, Scrunge
Suggestive Mark	Halo, Head and Shoulders, Born Blonde
Descriptive Mark	Double Bubble Gum, Sea and Ski, Sunlite, Turtle Wax

力魄之君强增
Dar-vos-á força e vigor
สร้างความแข็งแรงและ
ความกระฉับกระเฉงให้ท่าน
vous donnera force et vigueur

Fig. 1. *The Famous Guinness "Harp."* The Guiness "Harp" symbol connotes quality to the consumer.
Courtesy, *Guinness Museum, Dublin*

trademarks, from the design view, are among others, the Morton Salt Co.'s "Girl with the Umbrella", the H. J. Heinz logo and the Sherwin-Williams "Globe" (designed by George W. Ford).

In an article titled "The Cold War" appearing in *New York Magazine* (June 14, 1982), Bernice Kanner notes that "People who buy designer ice cream are buying image. They don't want the ordinary stuff; they want pretension—cachet and snob appeal. And ice-cream emperors are only too happy to serve it up, with phony, exotic names that obscure the unexotic places where it is made. The 'Rolls-Royce of ice cream', Frusen Gladje, despite its Swedish pretensions, is made in Utica, New York, the mock-Swiss Alpen Zauper in Brooklyn; and Häagen-Dazs, despite the map of Scandinavia on its package and its meaningless Danish-sounding name, is from Woodbridge, New Jersey. (Then again, London Fog raincoats are made in Baltimore, Vermont Maid syrup in New Jersey, and Philadelphia cream cheese in Wisconsin and New York. But that's another story.)"

In order to properly develop salable brand names, certain well-defined rules should be followed:

1. *The name should suggest something about the product's characteristics. It should describe the product without using ordinary English words.* Easy-Off (Boyle-Midway), Deep Cleanser (Avon Products, Inc), Beautyrest

Fig. 2. *Descriptive Name.*
The name PreSun aptly
describes the product's
function as a sunscreen.
Courtesy, *Westwood
Pharmaceuticals, Inc.*

(Simmons), Glade (S. C. Johnson and Co.) and Range-Toppers (Corning Glass Works) are examples of names that are both descriptive and functional. But who would know that Heavenly Hash is an ice cream, Good News, a disposable razor and Hi-Fi, a line of cosmetics?

2. *The name should be short, unique, easy to pronounce, spell and remember.* Excellent examples include the short one-syllable names such as Joy, Cheer, Fab, Tide, Gleem, Mum, Crest, Shout, Vel, Off and Pledge. The preference by the public for such names is why Budweiser became Bud, Lucky Strike became Luckies and Michelob became Mic! The names will also tend to be better remembered if they have a suggestive connotation. Old Grandad and Wild Turkey are excellent examples.

3. *All names selected should be distinctive and identify the specific product.* Brands such as Gold Medal, Blue Ribbon, Imperial or Mark I, II, III are not particularly suitable for the specific product or service. When motivational researcher Louis Cheskin suggested that A-1 beer be renamed Lancers A-1 beer, sales rapidly climbed for the Arizona Brewing Company. A name such as Whisker Lickins not only fits the product but probably wouldn't work for another kind of product.

4. *The name should be sufficiently versatile to be applicable to new products added to the product line.* The famous Maxwell House name has

been adapted to Max Pax premeasured coffee and Maxim freeze-dried coffee. Eastman Kodak conjugates its diverse product lines by reworking its name and initials, such as Ektachrome, Kodachrome and Kodacolor. Frigidaire is an excellent name for a refrigerator and other cold-image products. When General Motors expanded its line of home appliances and added Frigidaire kitchen ranges, the name lost some of its sales appeal. When Jeno Plaucci of Chun King fame introduced "Wilderness" brand fruit filling and added his name "Jeno's" on the label, testing quickly indicated that consumers objected to his name on the label and associated it with a greasy, spicy, pizza-like product.

5. *The name should have no unpleasant connotations.* A good name should not be antagonistic. Yves St. Laurent's brand name Opium might create a mood for its perfume, but it could be quite offensive to a sizeable percentage of potential customers who consider opium dangerous and illegal.

Fig. 3. *Corporate Line Extension.* The use of the Pathmark name on a wide variety of goods offers the consumer an assurance of quality on differing products.

Courtesy, *Supermarkets General, Inc.*

25

The brand Opium also triggered a protest from the Chinese community who regard real opium as an alien poison forced onto them by foreigners. Yankee Clipper brand alarm clocks did not sell well throughout the South but did sell when its trademark was changed to Dixie Bell. Soul brand beer, produced in 1967 by the Maier Brewing Corporation in Los Angeles, was considered to be an objectionable name by the National Association for the Advancement of Colored People. Their protest was so strong that the brands were withdrawn after two years on the market.

6. *The name should be capable of being used internationally.* The trademark selected might have a totally different meaning in some other language. Mikado pencils were widely sold in the U.S., however, after Pearl Harbor the Eagle Pencil Company changed its trademark to Mirado. There is even a confection sold in Denmark named Prick. A German paper tissue called Tempo, which means speed, when introduced in France was pronounced by most Frenchmen as Tampon, which of course is an altogether different kind of product. A brand of cigarettes named Windsor didn't make it in Denmark because that was the name of the leading toilet paper. It is not easy to pick a name that can be pronounced internationally, but concerns like Nescafe, Coca-Cola and Esso have done the trick and profited from it.
of a brand to be remembered as a picture is particularly valuable. There are a large number of very well known trademarks in active use—Shell's scallop shell, the Flying Red Horse of Socony, the Four Roses label, Robertson's golliwog and more. Even the shirt has become a veritable zoo! (see Table 1.3).

Simplicity is the keynote of a good trademark. Whatever form is used should be so simple in elements and execution that its poster quality will establish a definite and sustained impression. Required is a form that will not

TABLE 1.3

SHIRTS—ANIMAL TRADEMARKS

Brand	Animal Used as Trademark
Izod Lacoste	Alligator*
Ralph Lauren	Polo Horse
Giorgio Armani	Eagle
Tiger of Sweden	Tiger
J. C. Penney	Fox
Campus Sportswear	Tiger
Jordache	Horsehead
Munsingwear Grand Slam	Penguin

*First used about 1931 when French tennis pro Rene Lacoste was nicknamed "the Croc" for his speed.

26

lose its essential features no matter how small it may be.

A good mark is better when not controlled by the circle, square, diamond, triangle or other such usual shapes. Irregular shape registers a longer impression. The famous Fisher body mark would be much better if its rectangular frame were omitted.

8. *The name must be capable of being registered and legally protected under the Lanham Act and other statutory or common laws.* This is a rather obvious requirement. A Michigan brewer put out a beer under the name of Korr's. The Colorado-based Adolph Coors Co. took a dim view of this move, claiming (and winning the case) that the Korr's name and label infringed on the Coors beer name and label. But even though Philip Morris was first with its Marlboro Lite brand of cigarettes, a federal court ruled that R. J. Reynolds Tobacco Co. could continue to market its new brand, Winston Light. If not legally protected, some brand names may become generic and can be used by any firm. This occurs because of widespread use, lapsing legal protection, patent expiration and/or excellent advertising on the firm's part (see Table 1.4).

One is the increased use of "X" and "Z" in deriving product names. First there was only Xerox. Then some time later came Exxon.* Now there's Xoil, Xplor, Sci-Tex, Printronix, Kevex and Xicor and Xylogics.

X is the mark beside the dotted line, the symbol of love, death and hidden treasures. Inserted between two numbers, it causes them to multiply, yet it stands as well for unknown quantities. Now X has found a new function in the names of unknown corporate quantities that have set out in quest of wealth and treasure in energy and high technology.

"We like to see names that suggest a way-out futuristic product," says J.

TABLE 1.4

BRAND NAMES THAT ARE NOW GENERIC

linoleum
aspirin
celluloid
cellophane
formica
kerosene
nylon
shredded wheat
thermos

*The basic appeal of a name such as Exxon is that it says nothing and it means nothing. This is also true of Kodak.

27

Morton Davis, president of the D. H. Blair Company, the Wall Street broker-age firm. Mr. Davis is a founder of Xplor, a new oil exploration company. "Take a name like Xicor (pronounced Zycore) for instance," Mr. Davis said. "While it doesn't mean anything, it has a certain ring, a pizzazz and a fizzle to it."

Because of the paucity of meaningful names, executives have begun to invent words they hope will convey an alluring image and pique the curiosity of investors.

For much the same reason, the Z has begun to spread as in Zeus Energy and Zoe Products. And in a few cases companies are going further afield. Gene M. Amdahl, the I.B.M. emigre who founded the Amdahl Corporation, has founded a new company that he named Acsys Ltd. after abandoning several other possibilities.

"We finally thought we had one that was way out there," recalled Mr. Amdahl, "but we were beaten to the punch by a new start-up that had just applied for a license." Still, the final name, which stands for Amdahl Computer Systems, has been well received by investors both here and in Europe, Mr. Amdahl said.

Not all newborn companies accept the theory that mystery arouses investors. They put the hardsell right up front, as in Bellwether Exploration, Lyric Energy and Big Bonanza.

To further illustrate that no rule of marketing is beyond exception, just consider the astounding success of the J.M. Smucker Company. They capitalized on their rather unique name by advertising—"With a name like Smucker's it has to be good".

A name has psychological implications and is not used only for identification. New product failure because of the brand name is inexcusable marketing and indicates poor research, and in today's economy, neither factor can be tolerated in good business.*

TESTING NEW NAMES

During the last decade, a new industry has arisen devoted to the pre-testing of proposed trademarks. These tests often take the form of public surveys to determine consumer reaction to the new trademark. Research conducted recently by a leading New York advertising agency has determined the number of brand names the average consumer can recognize. It comes to a little over 1,000.

*Names are also changed. In 1981, a total of 572 U.S. corporations changed their names. This was up 36 percent from 1980.

Fig. 4. *New Era Potato Chips*. This dietetic snack not only promises a "New Era" for its consumers but also illustrates a slender woman on its package.
Courtesy, *Hercules, Inc.*

Ernest Dichter, a leader in the field of motivational research, relates how a brand name is tested.* In pre-screening a German laundry detergent, called Persil, his organization found that to most Spaniards who participated in the study, the name suggested a strong masculine product. This permitted the development of an advertising campaign in which the masculine sounding laundry detergent married the "feminine" linen waiting to be washed.

Opatow Associates, Inc. (919 Third Avenue, New York, New York) has developed a "1981 Packaging Impact Test." The test involves a consumer survey of packaging effectiveness to check many aspects of the package. One factor tested is product and brand imagery.

Other tests used are conducted by simply interviewing the particular segment of the buying public whose judgement is needed. This may be done on a door-to-door basis or randomly.

Because of the trend towards increasing consumerism, it is certain that the use of surveys in the merchandising of products will increase. It is also highly conceivable that they will be even more widely used to pre-test proposed marks as the search intensifies for "the Mark" that will outsell the competition.

REGISTRATION OF TRADEMARKS

Use in commerce is required for the registration of all trademarks. The mark must be displayed on a product, its package or an accompanying label, or it must be displayed in the sale or advertising of a service. A trademark need not be registered in order for it to be used in commerce. It must, how-

*In "Packaging: The Sixth Sense," Calners (1973).

ever, be registered if the user of the mark wishes to be regarded as its legal owner with exclusive rights to its use. The mark must also clearly indicate that it is registered for the user to have full legal protection.

One area of trademark law has recently become quite controversial. Large marketers obtain a trademark and then discontinue its use after initial use. Procter and Gamble, for example, is reported to have a stockpile of 60 trademarked names on hand for various products. This practice has been used as a ploy to "lock up" attractive names.

There are two registers in which a trademark may be registered, the Primary Register and the Supplemental Register. If a trademark is ineligible for the Primary Register, but has been in lawful use in commerce for the year preceding the filing of the application for registration, it may be registered on the Supplemental Register. Registration on the Supplemental Register does not give the right to prevent importation of goods bearing an infringing mark, but it does provide some protection to the owner by giving the right to sue in the United States Court.

TABLE 1.5

DESIGNER NAME VS. OTHER PRODUCTS

Designer	Products
Oscar de la Renta	Bedding, perfume, furs, scarves, eyeglass frames, jewelry, swimsuits.
Gloria Vanderbilt	Home furnishings
Pierre Cardin	Vast range of products—cars, jet airplanes, computers, clocks, backgammon sets, wine
Bill Blass	Candy, etc.
Sasson	Dresses, suits, scarves, fake furs, leather goods, swimwear, men's sport underwear, bras, panties, children's sportswear, belts, hosiery, dolls

Ordinarily, a trademark may not be registered if it merely describes goods or services or their geographical location, or if it consists primarily of a surname. However, if an applicant can prove that a mark has been in substantially exclusive and continuous use in commerce for 5 years preceding the application date, the mark may be registered in the Primary Register. A label design can qualify for trademark protection. There are several landmark cases involving labels including a polka-dot pattern on cans and the proportions and arrangements of red, white and blue stripes on a shaving cream can.

Once the mark is registered, the words "Registered in the U.S. Patent and Trademark Office'' or the letter R enclosed in a circle is used with it. If a trademark has been applied for, or a common-law trademark is claimed, the letters "TM" should be affixed in proximity to the element.

The application for registration of a trademark must be written in English, and it must include a drawing of the mark (on 8″ × 11″ white paper in India ink), five specimens or facsimiles (no longer than 8½″13″, and a $35.00 fee for registration in each class. There are 42 official classifications of goods and services, and applications must indicate the one or more that apply to the mark. For a list of official classifications, as well as other detailed requirements concerning the presentation and form of applications, and a complete schedule of fees, the Office of Patents and Trademarks, Washington, D.C. 20231, should be consulted.

The trademark division of the Patent and Trademark Office, has a Search Room in which a digest of registered marks is maintained, arranged according to classifications. The Search Room is open to the public, and it is advisable to check this digest before adopting a trademark to avoid possible conflict with previously registered marks.

The Trademark Office also has several publications (including a section on trademarks in the Official Gazette of the Patent Office, which may be purchased or subscribed to separately) and furnishes copies of registrations for a fee.

TABLE 1.6

BUILDING NAMES

Building	How named
1080—The Residence on Madison	identification with tradition by having a number
The Columbia (96th St. and Broadway, N.Y.C.)	near Columbia University, strength, longevity and a good rallying point for the community
The Piano Factory (454 W. 46th St., N.Y.C.)	named used by older residents of neighborhood and was a piano factory until 1930
The Courant, Mayfair Towers, Buckingham East, the Normandy, The Elysabeth, The Connaught, St. James Tower	British influence
Bland Houses	James Bland, noted black composer
Orwell House	George Orwell, noted literary figure

Trademark registration lasts for 20 years and is renewable for another 20 years for an additional fee. But, in the sixth year after the registration of a mark, a declaration of use must be filed. This declaration must show that the mark is still in use, or that if it is not, nonuse is not intended as complete abandonment of its use. The same rule applies to renewal.

In the U.K., the initial term of registration is seven years but the registration can be renewed indefinitely for further periods, each of 14 years.

ROYAL WARRANTS

Although not directly related to trademarks, the use of a royal coat of arms on a product often enhances both the prestige and sales volume of the specific item. It is the system formalized by the British Royal Family that is, perhaps, the most widely recognizable of all royal warrants.

More than 800 businesses now hold the right to boast acceptance by Queen Elizabeth, the Duke of Edinburgh, the Queen Mother and Prince Charles.* The origins of the royal warrant go back to the 12th centruy charters granted by monarchs to various guilds, but the practice did not flourish until Queen Victoria gave it a big push starting in 1837. She used more things and had more residences than the other monarchs. Queen Victoria eventually granted warrants to six different opticians, evidence that warrants are never regarded as exclusive.

Despite the multitude of suppliers to the various royal residences, the right to display a royal coat of arms on letterheads, pads, shops and/or packages is highly prized. The crown's endorsement is bestowed, not bought— the palace does not accept free samples or other lures. Export customers often like to feel they are buying quality merchandise that is recognized by the British royal house.

The list of warrant holders is published annually and provides, among other things, some idea of the scope of the royal business establishment as well as clues as to how the leading figures live.

There are, for example, suppliers of cattle-feeding equipment, tractors, forage, trucks and insecticides. In addition, an overwhelming variety of suppliers of domestic goods and services are represented, including those for strawberries, window-shade fabric, piano tuning, deodorizers, marmalade, bagpipes, potted shrimps, disposable tableware, floor polishers and more.

Once a company starts getting royal orders, it is not terribly hard to ob-

*Several Scandinavian nations have followed the lead of the U.K. and issue royal warrants. These include Norway, Denmark and Sweden.

Fig. 5. *Colman's Mustard.* Colman's Mustard products carry the royal warrant (note the mustard tin in the lower right corner). A special Warrant of Mustard to Her Majesty was conferred by Queen Victoria in 1866, and in 1868, a Warrant as purveyors to HRH the Prince of Wales.

Courtesy, *J & J Colman Ltd.*

tain the ultimate business cachet, the warrant. The basic requirement is that a company supply the royal household in a significant way for at least three years. (Provisions paid for by the Government, such as those for the Household Cavalry, do not count. Some allowance is made for big-ticket, infrequently purchased items, like an organ).

Then it is up to the company to apply for the warrant. Nobody will tell it to apply.

Although warrant holders are listed by company, the warrants are, in face, issued only to individuals. They run for ten years and are then automatically reviewed. Occasionally someone is dismissed for failing to abide by the strict rules under which appointments are made, such as using the warrant in advertising.

A tabulation in the early 1960's showed 42 warrant holders to be women, but their numbers are said to have fallen a bit since then. The warrant holders list shows only a handful of foreign companies—French champagne producers, a Bermuda art dealer, the Danish makers of Cherry Heering. Among the American names to appear are H. J. Heinz, Mobil, Kellogg, Parker Pen and Ford. But these warrants are issued through British subsidiaries. One can acquire a warrant by takeover, but the appointment cannot be passed "sideways" to a sister company or "up" to the corporate parent.

Foreign firms can apply as long as they supply products directly to the royal household; however, the warrant is essentially a British tradition.

Unsolicited goods sent to the royal household would normally be sent back and such an offer would not help a supplier in obtaining a warrant. Special discounts are not countenanced either.

It costs companies nothing to get a royal warrant, and the palace gets nothing out of it. The warrants are not granted for commercial purposes. It is

TABLE 1.7

MATCH THE STORE NAME WITH BUSINESS

Store Name	Type of Business		
DRESSED TO KILL	Discount poultry	Used clothing	Tuxedo rental
SACRED GROUNDS	Parochial bookstore	Coffee house	Univ. of San Fran. cafeteria
GROWING CONCERN	Barber shop	Furniture reproductions	Teen charm studio
PRUNE YOUR POPPY	Gardening service	Hair cutting	Clothing alterations
TIP TOE INN	Foot care	Deli	Meditation studio
HASBEANS	Used apparel	Coffee shop	Mexican food
SECONDS TO GO	Athletic shoes	Thrift shop	Clock repair
ENDANGERED SPECIES	Birds and pets	European/ Chinese artifacts	Exterminator
OLD GOLD	Coins/ metals	Classic artifacts	Antique jewelry
OFF THE WALL	Indoor tennis	Art dealer	Commercial painter

The correct category of each business shows in the center column.

From, Ralph C. Shaffer, "The Game in Names," New York Times June 6, 1982.

a stamp of approval, personal approval. Warrant holders may use the royal coat of arms in advertising but may not blatantly say "the Queen uses my soap". The warrant stands as a sort of seal, but nothing more. Never are they allowed to give any detail of what they supply to the royal household. Companies that served former royal households but no longer do may say, for example, that they supplied George VI, but may not use any coat of arms with it.

While the use of the warrant is usually quite desirable, it has, at least, one drawback. Many people see the coat of arms as somewhat foreboding and decide that the product or store must be too expensive for them and, perhaps, it might just put them off.

2
FROM CLAY TO CONTAINERS

"A Baker must set his owne proper marke upon every loafe of bread that hee maketh and selleth, to the end that if any bread be faultie in weight, it may bee then knowne in whom the fault is."
Bakers Marking Law
(England, 1266)

The use of trademarks predates written history. When man traded face to face, there was no need for a trademark. Once the trader's success spread outside his immediate area, he needed a mark to distinguish his product from others.

The urge by humans to differentiate and identify is basic. In Genesis, when Cain was expelled from the Garden of Eden after killing Abel, the Lord set a "mark" upon Cain. This derived from the already familiar practice of cattle branding practiced by the Egyptians and the inhabitants of early Bronze Age Europe.

The earliest identified markings on bricks and tiles date back to ancient Egypt. These bricks were often marked with the manufacturer's name, monarch's name and usually identified by a picture of the particular project for which they were intended. Nebuchadnezzar had his name stamped on every brick of his palace.

Chinese pottery bore a mark on its base noting the date manufactured, emperor's reign, maker's name and, often, its place of manufacture. Quarry marks and stonecutters signs are found in Phoenician projects and in the ruins of ancient Troy, Olympia and Damascus.

In ancient Greece and in the Roman Empire, trademarks were extensively used on many different types of products. They were used on amphorae, terra-cotta tiles, bricks, oil lamps, medicine containers and cheese jars. From the ruins in Pompeii and Herculaneum, archeologists have unearthed evidences of signboards on shops as well as markings on goods. Henry Sampson, in his pioneering work, "History of Advertising" published in London (1875), says that "as luxury increased, and the number of houses or shops dealing in the same article multiplied, something more was wanted. Particular trades continued to be confined to particular streets; the desideratum then was to give to each shop a name or token by which it could be mentioned in conversation—thus a hare and a bottle stood for Harebottle, and two cocks for Cox. Others whose names could represent, adopted pictorial objects; and as the quantity of these augmented, new subjects were continually required. The animal kingdom was ransacked, from the mighty elephant to the humble bee, from the eagle to the sparrow; the vegetable kingdom, from the palm tree and cedar to the marigold and daisy; everything on the earth and in the firmament above it was put under contribution." Here then are the first traces of the use of trademark symbols and the now common use of both animals and other objects to denote brands.

From the fall of the Roman Empire to about the fourteenth century, western mankind lived through a time known as the Dark Ages, which was characterized by a decline of learning. During this period, the use of marks virtually disappeared. Artisans and tradesmen were unable to read or write even the simplest types of inscriptions.

The first mark to emerge out of the abysmal ignorance of the Dark Ages was the personal mark, which identified individuals. There were also house marks that identified the family living there. Packages and goods were also marked, especially when they were to be shipped considerable distances.

Fig. 6. *Wine Bottle (1725).* This bottle has a seal marked P. Bastard 1725. Bottles of this type were popular between 1710 and 1728. Courtesy, *John Harvey and Sons Ltd.*

There is a recorded case of a shipwreck in which balls of wax were recovered. The merchants who had shipped them were able to recover their salvaged property by the proprietary marks that appeared on their goods.

Other marks appearing in the Middle Ages included watermarks on paper, marks on cloth, printers marks, marks on pottery, glass bottles, apothecary jars* and even on bells.

In the Middle Ages, large quantities of guild marks also were used to enforce control of industry, especially territorial trade barriers. Every trade was regulated by its guild, which controlled prices and standards of work. The Guild's officers regularly and carefully inspected the work of members, because dishonest workmen could give the trade a bad name. Marks were often used to denote guild approval and certification. Typical marks were used by guilds on wine, knives, swords, drapes, pottery and precious metals.

Silver marks (hallmarks) were some of the most commonly used marks in the Middle Ages, especially in England. The history of silver hallmarking began in 1238, when as a result of fraudulent practices by manufacturing goldsmiths, Henry III attempted to control standards for silver and gold products. He decreed that six goldsmiths of the City of London be selected to supervise the craft, and laid down standards of fineness for both metals.

In 1300, Edward I reiterated his father's ordinance, commanding firstly, that silver be no worse than the "sterling" standard, and additionally that it be marked with the King's mark of the leopard's head. Other marks soon followed. In 1363, an ordinance of Edward III empowered every goldsmith to have his own maker's mark. Much of modern trademark law and many common-law rules concerning trademarks are similar to the initial guild legislation.

It was the guild mark that evolved into the trademark in the modern sense when goods began to be shipped for long distances. Preferences for particular workmanship developed and the trademark on the product allowed the consumer to identify the product with its maker.

MODERN TRADEMARKS EMERGE

The industrial revolution finally catalyzed the widespread use of trademarks in the modern sense. With increased advertising came growth in distribution. A method was soon needed to identify the source of the goods and trademarks appeared to "fit the bill."

*An excellent three-part series of articles on early English apothecaries drug jars appears in: *Art and Antiques*, March 13, 20 and 27, (1981). Written by Dr. John F. Wilkenson, it describes the various marks present in these early jars.

TABLE 2.1

EARLY TRADEMARK NAMES

Date	Name
1706	Crosse & Blackwell—introduced in U.S. in 1826
1715	Old Medford Brand Rum
1759	Wedgwood
1768	Encyclopedia Brittanica
1769	Gordon's Gin
1770	Spode
1780	Baker's Chocolate
1797	Keiler's Dundee Marmalade
1817	Mallory hats
1824	Angostura Bitters
1845	Burnett's Vanilla
1847	International Silvers "Rogers Bros" brand
1854	Booth's Fish
1855	Babbit's Lye (first to put soap in wrapper)
1857	Robert Burns Cigars
1857	Eagle Brand Condensed Milk

Trademarks were occasionally used in the United States before the Revolutionary War. But their use dramatically increased after the Civil War (see Table 2.1). Aided by the widespread use of outdoor advertising during the war, the first federal trademark law was passed in 1870, but only 10 years later was declared unconstitutional because it was thought to restrict commerce between the states.

Although a new law was passed in 1881, the original 1870 law was responsible for the first trademark registered in the United States. The honor

Fig. 7. *The Underwood "Devil"*. Underwood's "Little Red Devil" was the first registered trademark for food.

Courtesy, *William Underwood & Co.*

39

Fig. 8. *The Famous Bass "Triangle."* The world famous Bass Red Triangle was originally a shipping mark.

Courtesy, *Bass Ltd.*

Fig. 9. *The Earliest Known Bass Label.* This label dating from before 1840 contains the Bass signature.

Courtesy, *Bass Ltd.*

went to the Averill Paint Company of New York who registered an eagle on October 25, 1870. Six years later, in 1876, the William Underwood Co. of Boston became the first firm to register a trademark for food—Underwood's Deviled Ham in the can with the "Little Red Devil." In the same year, the Bass Brewing Co., Ltd. registered the first trademark in England (the famous Bass red triangle).*

Brand names were rapidly transforming the face of American business. From 121 registered trademarks in 1871 and 1,000 in 1875, more than 10,000 were registered in 1906. And the use of trademarks kept growing (more than

---

*It is said that a representative of Bass spent the night on the steps of the registrar's office to be sure of getting first place in the Trademarks Register. Bass registered three of their bottle labels and then the triangle and diamond on the labels which were always red.

700,000 are registered today).

During the latter part of the 19th century, the patent medicine field contributed widely to the growth of trademarks in the United States. Even before registration began in 1870, the fiercely competitive patent medicine industry made judicial history in this area.

PATENT MEDICINE TRADEMARKS

Unwilling to patent their medicines, these pre-1906 patent medicine manufacturers coined a wide variety of trade names for their products. Patent issuance meant that the product formulation became known to the public, although this was the last thing the businessman of medicine had on his mind, since his products were "secrets" or nostrums, literally "ours." If most of these useless formulations were known they would be immediately recognized as being dangerous or at least useless. A trade name, indicating the brand but not the product and registered with the U.S. patent office, was capable of a stout defense under the trademark laws without any product disclosure. These patent medicines technically enjoyed government protection; the contents of the medicine remained secret.

The impact of repetition was further strengthened if the product name was memorable (see Table 2.2). Some medicine hucksters turned to allitera-

TABLE 2.2

PRE-1906 PATENT MEDICINE TRADENAMES

Variety Group	Examples
Doctor	Dr. Ayer's Hair Vigor, Dr. Parmenter's Magnetic Oil, Dr. Flint's Quaker Bitters, Dr. C. Y. Girard's Ginger Brandy, Dr. Grosvenor's Belanodyne Porous Plaster, Dr. A. L. Taylor's Oil of Life, Dr. Hooker's Cough and Croup Syrup, Dr. Jordan's Balsam of Rakasiri.
Indian	Indian Compound of Honey, Boneset and Squills, Ka-Fon-Ka, Dr. Morse's Indian Root Pills, Dr. Kilmer's Indian Cough Cure, Kickapoo, Modoc Oil, Seminole Cough Balsam, Nez Perce Catarrah Snuff, Wright's Indian Vegetable Pills.
Chinese	Dr. Lin's Celestial Balm of China, Dr. Drake's Canton Chinese Hair Cream, Carey's Chinese Catarrah Cure, Ching's Patent Worm Lozenges.
Religion	St. Anne, St. Joseph, Pastor Koenig, Father John, Balm of Gilead, Paradise Oil, Resurrection Pills, 666, St. Jacob's Oil.
Women	7 Sutherland Sisters Hair Grower, Lydia E. Pinkham's Vegetable Compound, Madame Dean's French Female Pills.

41

tion with product names such as Burdock's Blood Bitters, Radway's Ready Relief, Swift's Sure Specific and Fechter's Famous Faricon. Others used names that reflected the cure offered—Dr. Adam's Wart Cure, Dent's Toothache Gum, Dr. Sweet's Infallible Liniment and Warner's Safe Cure. These names were often printed with a distinctive type inducing a feeling of familiarity. Pictorial symbols served the same function, such as Radway's ministering angel and Lydia Pinkham's maternal countenance (registered in 1876). While the formula of the medicine might change over time, the trademark endured protected first by common law and, after 1870, by federal statute. Until the Pure Food and Drugs Act of 1906 established initial control over proprietary remedy promotion, the nostrum producers were free to mix whatever they wanted. It all ended in 1906 but trademarks had already become "part and parcel" of American life.

Smith Brothers Cough Drops

The introduction of Smith Brothers Cough Drops is yet another landmark in the trademark history of the late 19th century. The product was originally called James Smith & Sons Compound of Wild Cherry Cough Candy. In 1866 the company passed on to James' sons, William and Andrew. The brothers changed the name of their product to Smith Brothers Cough Drops and were enjoying huge success when competitors introduced products with similar names such as Schmitt Brothers, Smythe Sisters or Smith and Bros. To protect their product, the brothers devised a distinctive trademark. Both brothers put their pictures on the large glass bowls placed in store windows from which the drops were sold, and then put into envelopes for the customer. By pure chance, the word "Trade" appeared under the picture of William and the word "Mark" under Andrew.

Fig. 10. *Lunch Box Style Tobacco Tin.* This American tin, circa 1895, conveys an interesting slogan, "Just Suits," as its trademark.
Courtesy, *U.S. Tobacco Museum*

The glass bowl container and the envelopes had definite limitations and in 1872 these two ingenious brothers developed one of the first uniform "factory-filled" packages. They put their cough drops into printed paperboard boxes each decorated with their now-famous trademark.

Until the 1890's, most American trademarks reflected patriotism and a sense of Victorian allegorical beauty. When immigration became an accepted part of American life, the trademark became identified with the product's attributes. Fewer people could read and a sense of familiarity was needed to convey the product to the consumer. People, figures, animals, comic types and slogans were introduced to the now rapidly consuming public.

TABLE 2.3

ORIGINS OF VICTORIAN TRADENAMES

Brand Name	Origin
Hovis (bread)	from "Hominis Vis"
Bovril (beef extract)	from "bos" (Latin for ox) and "vril," from Vrilya, the name given to the "life force" in Bulwer-Lytton's lesser known novel, *The Coming Race*, published in 1871.
Worcestershire Sauce (Lea & Perrins)	first produced commercially by Lea & Perrins in the city of Worcester in 1837. First served in a Worcester chop-house.
Mellin's Emulsion	from Gustav Mellin, the infant food manufacturer
1 – Dewar's	1 – Thomas R. Dewar
2 – Bell's	2 – Arthur and Robert Bell
3 – Teachers	3 – William Teacher
4 – John Walker	4 – John Walker
5 – Haig	5 – John Haig

Uneeda Biscuits

The 19th century ended with the *one* biggest landmark event in the history of American trademarks—Nabisco's huge success with "Uneeda" biscuits. *Fortune* magazine later said that the National Biscuit Company "did almost as much as the introduction of canned foods before it, and the invention of the electric refrigerator after it to change the techniques of modern advertising." Nabisco was instrumental in establishing the concept of brand names and had chosen "a little child to lead them" out of the cracker barrel age and into the modern era of packaged trademarked foods.

43

N.W. Ayer and Son advertising agency was responsible for the product name "Uneeda Biscuit,"* and a trademark was soon needed to reflect the unique product—prepackaged soda crackers. The task fell to a young copywriter named Joseph J. Geisinger. He first thought of a fisherman, clad in a slicker, eating dry biscuits out of a dry package, an interesting concept which made the point that Nabisco products were always fresh and crisp. But the fisherman concept did not appeal to Adolphus W. Green, one of the founders of the National Biscuit Company.

Geisinger happened to have a five-year-old nephew named Gordon Stille, a plump-cheeked, bright-eyed boy with a winsome look. His uncle asked him whether he would be willing to pose for an advertising photographer, dressed in boots, oil hat and slicker, with a box of "Uneeda" biscuits under his arm. The child agreed. So did his parents. Pictures were taken and the rest is history.

When Adolphus Green saw the proofs, he was enthusiastic. The pictures appeared to have the human quality needed to appeal to the consuming public. In a short time, the portrait of the boy in the slicker clutching the "Uneeda" biscuit box became one of the most widely used advertising motifs in the history of the advertising business.

It was also at the turn of the century that National Biscuit Company took its first important step toward creating its "coat of arms."

As the basic element, Nabisco used a symbol that had an ancient origin. A similar design has been found in the Great Pyramid at Giza, and in the early Christian era, the circle and cross with two bars was used to represent the

TABLE 2.4

TRADEMARK INFRINGEMENTS—"UNEEDA" NAME *

Name	Date
Iwanta	Injunction won (1899) by NBC
Uwanta	Injunction won (1899) by NBC
Ulika Bis-Kit	Injunction won (1904) by NBC
I-lika	Injunction won (1908) by NBC
Eta Hargrave Biscuit	Injunction won (1909) by NBC

*Calkins and Holden in *Modern Advertising* (1908) say, "The imitation of the coined word "Uneeda" has been slavish, unreasonable, short-sighted and stupid."

*On Sept. 6, 1898, the name "Uneeda" was selected by Adolphus Green from a list of potential names submitted for his approval by Henry N. McKinney of N. W. Ayer and Son. It was registered with the U.S. Patent Office on December 27, 1898 (see Table 2.3).

triumph of the moral and spiritual over the evil and material. During the 15th century, the symbol was used as a printer's mark by the Society of Printers in Venice.

In 1900, Adolphus Green, familiar with the history of this symbol, suggested that it be incorporated in a "coat of arms" for the company.

The Nabisco "coat of arms" went through a number of changes from 1900 to the present, but the basic design and symbol stayed much the same. The present Nabisco "coat of arms" is a red triangular seal which spans the upper left-hand corner of Nabisco packages.

Exactly how the National Biscuit Company revolutionized and dramatically altered the "American way of life" can be understood by reading contemporary observers.

In Calkins and Holden's *Modern Advertising* published in 1909, just 11 years after "Uneeda Biscuits" first came onto the shelf, "Uneeda's" impact is fully sketched:

> Take, for instance, the soda biscuit. Formerly it was supplied loose, in bulk from a barrel, from which the grocer weighed out the necessary quantity. The method was uncleanly and unsanitary, and crispness was lost. It required an unnecessary number of handlings which took time and were distasteful. The name, soda-biscuit, meant several kinds of biscuit in bulk; the customer seldom knew them apart; the most intelligent thing she could do was to point them out.
>
> Today, the same housewife is familiar with the name of a biscuit in a package, wrapped first in a sanitary, waxed, air-and moisture-proof wrapper, then in a compact, handy carton, and finally in a decorative wrapper. This package would now be recognized by a large percentage of the population of the United States at a glance. The housewife simply gives to the grocer the name of that particular biscuit; and the grocer takes down the package.
>
> Five years ago no one thought of asking for a cracker or soda-biscuit by name. To-day, one company (National Biscuit Company) has made its products household words.

3
FORGOTTEN TRADEMARKS
OF THE PAST

There's a face that haunts me ever,
There are eyes mine always meet;
As I read the morning paper,
As I walk the crowded street.

Ah! She knows not how I suffer!
Her's is now a world-wide fame,
But 'til death that face shall greet me.
Lydia Pinkham is her name.
                    Dartmouth Song (ca. 1885)

From about 1880 on, scores of fascinating new product trademarks emerged onto the American scene. Laced with hungry and energetic immigrants, the United States of the 1880's till about World War I was a vital and growing market.

In *The Americans: The Democratic Experience*, Daniel J. Boorstin states that brand names "drew together in novel ways people who might not otherwise have been drawn together at all—people who did not share a religious or political ideology, who were not voyaging together on the prairie nor building new towns. The peculiar importance of American consumption communities made it easier to assimilate, to 'Americanize', the many millions who arrived here in the century after the Civil War."

Replacing the allegorical symbols and fancy label characteristic of the very early trademarks came scores of newer trademarks—all designed to add familiarity to the product. Many of these trademarks still exist and are quite successful—Aunt Jemima, Baker's Chocolate Waitress, Psyche, The White Rock Girl, and the Old Dutch Cleanser Woman. Still more have been discarded or modified with time. Who can remember the cleanser Sapolio,

46

Fig. 11. *The Old Dutch Cleanser Woman.* Originally a goosegirl in a painting at the home of a Cudahy Packing Company official, her briskly hostile posture was ideally suited to the slogan "Chases Dirt."
Courtesy, *Werbin and Morrill, Inc.*

Lydia Pinkham's face, the Bull Durham "bull" or the famous Burma-Shave jingles? In passing, from the scene, trademarks such as these, as well as many others, have left their indelible mark in the ranks of all presently used trademarks.

Sapolio

In Spotless Town they got a bore
Who slyly spat upon the floor
They washed his mouth as white as snow
With water and Sapolio.
If you don't expect his fate
You must not expectorate.
Early Advertising Sign

The first commercial scouring powder of abrasive ever manufactured in the United States was a premium-priced product called Sapolio.* The name was one of the first commercial examples of a "coined" name (Kodak was introduced years later in 1885).

Sapolio was introduced in 1869 by Enoch Morgan Sons, a company with a long soap making history. Enoch Morgan died in 1853 and his eldest son, John Williams Morgan, took over the business. When he was 21, he pur-

*Sapolio contained quartz, which was finely ground and bonded with conventional soap. It was used mainly for heavy scouring on greasy sinks, stoops and marble tabletops. The quartz came from farmers, who became miners when they found outcroppings of the mineral on their land.

chased the business and later took into partnership his brothers, William Henry and George Frederick Morgan.

Advertising was one of the basic reasons for the success of Sapolio. From an initial expenditure of $30,000 per year in 1870 to over $350,000 in 1910, Sapolio's popularity was the result of the advertising genius of Artemus Ward, son of the famous humorist. Ward started working for Enoch Morgan Sons in 1869 and was one of the best known advertising men of the time. He was a director of the firm, owner of *Fame*, an advertising newspaper, and was deeply involved in a wide variety of additional advertising projects.

When Sapolio was first introduced, it was a genuinely new product, replacing the imported English product "Bath Brick." People had to be educated to its use, and many novel and elaborate advertising stunts were tried before it achieved its eventual success. In 1892, Capt. Andrews single handedly sailed from Atlantic City, New Jersey to Spain to repay Columbus's visit. But Sapolio's greatest success came about in 1900 when the firm introduced its Spotless Town trademark. Spotless Town jingles, written by James K. Fraser, were probably the first successful advertising verses. They told the story of the citizens of Spotless Town and, in a sense, created a Mother Goose

Fig. 12. *Sapolio Advertisement.* This turn-of-the-century ad features Sapolio as a blend of patriotism and national pride.

Courtesy, *Smithsonian Institution*

world for adults.

The jingles had great popularity and were quoted everywhere. They became the basis for political cartoons in newspapers and were the forerunner of the modern advertising verse. The trademark and the product became so well known that "Sapolio," like "Victrola," could almost be considered a common noun. About the time of World War I, Sapolio ceased its advertising and today is no longer on the market.

Lydia Estes Pinkham

Mrs. Jones of Walla Walla,
Mrs. Smith from Kan Ka Kee,
Mrs. Cohn, Mrs. Murphy,
Sing your praises lustily,
Refrain: OH-H-H, we'll sing of Lydia Pinkham,
And Her love for the human race.
How she sells her vegetable compound,
And the papers, the papers they publish,

They publish her FACE!
Pinkham Ballad ca. 1890

Perhaps the most colorful promotional methods of the Victorian era are associated with a prim Victorian lady named Mrs. Lydia E. Pinkham of Lynn, Mass. When she died in 1883, she was rich, respected, famous and an enthusiastic member of the W.C.T.U. But her greatest fame was still to come! Within a decade after her death, her portrait was known to millions of consumers and was often confused with the likeness of Queen Victoria, Sarah Bernhardt and even President Cleveland's new bride.

Lydia E. Pinkham was born on February 9, 1819 in Lynn, Mass., the daughter of a shoemaker. She married Issac Pinkham in 1843, reared a family, did some nursing and, in 1875, first produced the herb remedy that made her face famous.

In about 1855, Issac received a recipe for an herb formula purported to cure "female complaints" as partial payment for an old debt. (He had endorsed a note for a Lynn machinist named George C. Todd and when Todd defaulted, Pinkham paid $25 on the note. In partial payment Todd gave Pinkham the formula.) In 1875, when the Pinkham family was in dire financial straits, Lydia started to produce, for sale, the medicine she had already been mixing in small lots for both her friends and family.

It was a modest beginning. The children filled bottles and folded circulars. Lydia made the medicine and Issac folded and bundled the pamphlets for distribution to the retail outlets. The family somehow selected the name

49

"Lydia E. Pinkham's Vegetable Compound" for their product. In 1876 Lydia registered her trademark and label with the U.S. Patent Office. Lydia wrote intimate and emotional handbills stressing the beneficial aspects of the medicine while always promoting the word "vegetable." "Yours for Health" soon became the product's slogan.

Many years later, the name selected proved to be a fortunate choice. When the government forced Lydia's competitors to change the name of their products to meet the truth-in-advertising standards of the twentieth century, the Pinkhams were beyond reproach.

Lydia's first labels were not particularly distinguished. They were descriptive and informative but lacked the aesthetic qualities necessary to capture consumer appeal. In 1879, Daniel Rogers Pinkham, Lydia's second child, had an idea that made advertising history!

Daniel decided to put a picture of a "healthy woman" on playing cards. When he came home for Christmas and saw his mother, he realized that he had found his "healthy woman." At sixty, Lydia E. Pinkham was a dignified, handsome woman with a benign maternal countenance. After a family meeting, Lydia posed for the photograph that would later appear on countless ads and bottle labels.

Lydia's fame quickly spread far and wide. It lasted as the firm's trademark for over 100 years. In 1968 the Lydia E. Pinkham Medicine Company was sold to Cooper Laboratories, a large and diversified pharmaceutical firm. The product is still made and bottled in Cooper's Puerto Rico plant and manages to gross over $700,000 annually. Lydia's face still appears on the outer carton; however, to a new generation, she is certainly hardly the famous personality that generations of previous consumers recognized!

Fig. 13. *Lydia E. Pinkham.* The famous Lydia Estes Pinkham pose that has appeared on millions of labels.

Courtesy, *Schlesinger Library, Radcliffe College*

Bull Durham

"None Genuine Without The Bull on Each Package"
Tag on Early Bull Durham
Pouch ca. 1890

One of the most recognized U.S. trademarks was registered on January 3, 1871 as trademark number 122—the "Durham Bull."

It all began somewhere around 1858 when the North Carolina Railroad was laid across the farm of Dr. Bartlett Durham, in Orange County, North Carolina. Named Durham Station, the small town eventually became the home of a tobacco company, blacksmith, tavern and several families. The Civil War brought Durham Station prosperity and its small tobacco industry grew larger and larger.

In 1860, Morris and Wright established another tobacco factory in Durham Station that principally manufactured plug tobacco, but utilized the clippings and waste tobacco by putting them in little bags and disposing of it as smoking tobacco. When war broke out, Wright sold his interest to his partner and joined the Confederate Army. J.R. Green then bought out the firm and became the successor to the business of Morris and Wright.

Green's business rapidly grew because of his product's popularity with both the Union soldiers under the command of Sherman and the Confederate soldiers under Johnston's command. (Durham was located close to the site where negotiations for Gen. Joseph E. Johnston's surrender to Gen. William T. Sherman took place.) After the war, orders came from all parts of the Union for "smoking tobacco in the small bags." Green soon needed a new name and trademark to identify both his novel product and package. His pre-war name, "Best Flavored Spanish Smoking Tobacco" seemed outdated.

He adopted as his brand name the words, "Genuine Durham Smoking Tobacco," and in one of the earliest applications of an animal as a trademark, he used the figure of a shorthorn Durham bull to represent the word "Durham" in 1866. His idea was suggested by the bull's head on Colman's Mustard, made in Durham England.* When Green died in 1869, William T. Blackwell became the firm's owner and registered and protected the bull trademark in long and costly litigation.

On Green's factory was placed a full-size painting of the bull (this was soon to become larger and automatic) in full view of the railroad, and as an advertisement of his business to all travelers. The town of Durham soon came to be associated with the picture as the "Home of the Bull."

Bull Durham's popularity (over 2 million pounds were sold in 1881),

*The earliest record of the use of the Bull's Head as Colman's trademark dates back to 1855.

51

caused a barnful of imitators to spring up. There were "Sitting Bull Durham," "Jersey Bull," "Black Bull," "Old Bull," "Bull's Head" and many others.

Later, the Bull Durham factory, under the brilliant leadership of Blackwell, was equipped to process 20,000 pounds of tobacco a day. An enormous bull, painted on paneled sheet iron, decorated the front of the building and the factory's steam whistle, by means of a mechanical gadget, imitated the bellow of a bull. Each bellow, it was said, cost six dollars and could be clearly heard thirteen miles away. The bull was the masterpiece of J. Gilmer Kerner, eccentric and temperamental artist, whose sign painting nom de plume was "Reuben Rink." Raging and triumphant, Reuben Rink's bulls seemed to paw the ground and emit flame from their nostrils. Eventually they appeared on barns and boulders and billboards throughout the country, even in Europe and the Near East. Reuben Rink is credited with the catch-phrase description of Durham as the "Town Renowned the World Around."

The Bull Durham brand is now owned by the American Tobacco Company. The words "The American Tobacco Co., Successor" were added to the label after James Buchanan Duke, the company's founder, acquired Blackwell's business in the 1890's.

Bull Durham followed the settlers to the West, became a favorite of Americans in the East and, in general, saw its popularity spread around the world with vigorous momentum. An advertisement proclaimed it "The Standard of the World." In the West a sack of "makin's" shared with a stranger on a lonely trail became a token of friendship . . . and to refuse a man a hand-rolled "Bull" was equal to an insult.

In the early days of the new frontier, Bull Durham was also used as a land measure. Buyer and seller would roll up their cigarettes, light them and start

Fig. 14. *"A Remarkable Bull."* The famous "Bull Durham" tobacco was made by the old W.T. Blackwell Durham Tobacco Co., Durham, N.C. Although quite famous in pouches, the tobacco was also packed in one-of-a-kind upright pocket tins. These designs varied slightly—from a hand pouring tobacco into a rolling paper, with the reverse showing the bull, to a later pack featuring the bull as a lithographed tag and a reverse picturing American Tobacco's (the successor firm to Blackwell) familiar Indian trademark.

Courtesy, *Werbin and Morrell, Inc.*

52

riding. The end of their smoke marked a distance of land in the transaction.

Many notables of yesteryear were devotees of "Bull" Durham, among them such famous men of letters as Henry Wadsworth Longfellow, Thackeray, James Russell Lowell and the English poet, Alfred Lord Tennyson. Thomas Carlyle, the famous British historian, smoked "Bull" Durham tobacco through "a yard of clay" (pipe). Indicating that "Bull" Durham was a favorite in all walks of life, a 1914 advertisement was headlined "The Democracy of 'The Makings'."

After World War I, Bull Durham gave way gradually to "tailor-made" cigarettes, only to be revived again by the Depression. It was advertised on 24-sheet posters as the 5-cent smoke, and headlines proclaimed, "Roll your own and save your 'Roll'." Sales jumped from 6 million pounds in 1930 to over 15 million pounds in 1932. The increase alone was enough to make 7½ billion cigarettes. Among the advertisements was the famous "Her Hero" ad, showing a cow casting an admiring glance in the direction of the intrepid "Bull."

The muslin bags with the bull-headed tags were still going strong in 1940 when nearly 20 million pounds, enough for 17 billion roll-your-owns, were sold. At a nickel a sack, the "Bull" was equivalent to 33 cigarettes in the hands of a dextrous roller.

Skilled rollers still abound, particularly in the South and West, and each year these smokers account for the sale of many thousands of pounds of Genuine "Bull" Durham.

The year 1966 marked the Bull's one-hundredth anniversary. But rather than being put out to pasture, he was being rejuvenated as Bull Durham Extra Size, the cigarette that "smokes slower for better taste."

Bull Durham is still being manufactured in limited distribution throughout the South. It is difficult to locate in most retail outlets, but like Lydia Pinkham's Vegetable Compound refuses to die and still enjoys a certain degree of popularity—even after 115 years!

Herpicide

"Going! Going!! Gone!!!"
Herpicide Trademark

So popular has been Herpicide's trademark, "Going! Going!! Gone!!!," that the phrase "Too late for Herpicide" became widely used in the English language.

When Dr. Newbro coined the trademark for his dandruff germ remedy, Newbro's Herpicide, he certainly did not foresee exactly how he would change the face of American advertising.

When the product first appeared, there was very little censorship on false and misleading advertising. Many manufacturers of hair and scalp preparations were exploiting their products to the gullible public. by extravagant statements. Dr. Newbro believed that in order to combat the unfair practices of his competitors, the keynote for his advertising should be "truth." He put emphasis on the fact that his remedy would save hair rather than grow hair, and his slogan told the story of hair and scalp neglect.

As soon as Dr. Newbro's product began to be marketed with his slogan, most of the unscrupulous advertisers disappeared. In all, Herpicide lasted over 50 years on the market, and it is remembered for its pioneering slogan in trademark history.

Burma - Shave

Within this vale /
Of toil and sin /
Your head grows bald /
But not your chin /
Burma-Shave.
Burma-Shave Jingle
(ca. 1935)

In the early 1920's, Clinton Odell was engaged in the process of manufacturing a liniment whose formula was supposed to have come from an old sea captain. The essential oils used in the liniment came from Burma and Malay; Odell combined the word "Burma" with the Latin word "vita" (for life) and called his new firm Burma-Vita.

Burma-Vita's main product was the basic liniment. Although it was a fairly popular product, its strong odor kept many consumers away. Another product was rapidly needed to keep the business profitable. The idea for the new product came from an English brushless shaving cream called "Lloyd's Euxesis." A brushless shaving cream was preferable to the use of a shaving brush and soap because it eliminated the problem of mildew. From "Lloyd's Euxesis" came the idea of a brushless shaving cream for Americans, and since the company was already called Burma-Vita, Burma-Shave seemed like a natural extension. Now the problem was how to convince the American male to accept the revolutionary brushless shaving cream!

Allan Odell, son of the founder, Clinton Odell, was mulling the situation over while he was driving along a country highway and saw a series of signs extolling the virtues of a filling station a short distance down the road. If the idea could work for a station, it could also work for Burma-Shave. The automobile age was just beginning and a new technique was needed to capture the imagination of the consumer. Risking $200 for the first set of road signs, Odell's first jingles appeared in 1926 on U.S. Highway 65 near Lakeville, Minn. Allan wrote the first:

Cheer Up /
Face /
The War /
Is Over

Allan and his younger brother, Leonard, installed these new signs. They used 18″ × 40″ boards spaced about 100 feet apart along the highway to advertise their shaving cream. A family driving by at 35 MPH had three seconds to reach each of the six signs displaying the jingle. Leonard drove a truck loaded with freshly painted signs while Allan raced ahead in a car and made a deal with farmers willing to rent the space. The $200 gamble soon paid off. Sales dramatically increased. By 1940, as Burma-Shave gained momentum

TABLE 3.1

TYPICAL BURMA-SHAVE JINGLES

A peach	Are your whiskers	Henry the Eighth
Looks good	When you wake up	Prince of Friskers
With lots of fuzz	Tougher than	Lost five wives
But man's no peach	A two-bit steak	But kept
And never was		His whiskers
Soon shaving brushes	Beneath this stone	The answer to
Will be trimmin	Lies Elmer Gush	A maiden's
Those screwey hats	Tickled to death	Prayer
We see	By his	is not a chin
One women	Shaving brush	of stubby hair
	Burma-Shave	Burma Shave
Past schoolhouses	Rip a fender	He played
Take it slow	off your car	A Sax
Let the little	Send it in	Had no B. O.
Shavers	For a half-pound jar	But his whiskers scratched
Grow		So she let him go
Don't take a curve	Free, free	If a trip to Mars
At 60 per	A trip	You'd earn
We hate to lose	To Mars	Remember, friend
A Customer	For 900 empty jars	There's no return

and its distribution increased, over 40,000 individual signs were in position.

Every sign and every jingle was recorded and filed by the Odell's secretary, Fidelia Dearlove. She kept track of the special Burma-Shave trucks, each with the words "Cheer Up" on their side panel, and she knew by heart where every jingle was located (see Table 3.1).

Burma-Shave sales grew rapidly after the World War II until about 1958 when the superhighway came into its own. High speed cars, the development of the electric razor and the popularity of the aerosol can for shaving cream all spelled the end of the Burma-Shave cream jar. In 1964, Burma-Shave sold out to Philip Morris who subsequently sold the division to the American Safety Razor Co. Burma-Shave cream is still being made for limited distribution, but their road signs are gone.

Few American advertisers ever received as much acceptance for their ads as did Burma-Shave. The spacing of the signs enforced a particular reading pace and even the most alert passenger could not read ahead to the punch line. Everyone in the car read and enjoyed it simultaneously. Burma-Shave's admirers said, "If a verse could be serialized in such a fashion, why not a short story—or even 'Gone With The Wind' for transcontinental driving?"* Burma-Shave's uniqueness inspired many new billboards along the nation's highways. When the signs died, a memorable piece of Americana was buried alongside them in their grave.**

The Gold Dust Twins

"Gold Dust. . . .used black children as their trademark and cashed in on old-fashioned stereotypes of blacks in menial positions and black children as 'pickaninnies'."

The Promise and the Product
(1979)

Of all the Black trademarks that were used for product identification, the "Gold Dust Twins" was one of the most widely recognizable.

Registered in 1884 by the N.K. Fairbank Company, it helped propel a washing powder into becoming a national favorite. Women everywhere, especially new brides, were constantly urged to "let the Gold Dust Twins" do your work. This soon became a familiar slogan and was persistently employed well into the first decades of our own century.

*In *The Shocking History of Advertising* by E.S. Turner
**An excellent work covering the complete Burma-Shave history is: Rowsome, Frank, *Verse By The Side of The Road*, Stephen Greene Press, Brattleboro, Vt. (1965)

Gold Dust Washing Powder was manufactured by the N.W. Fairbank Company, Chicago, Ill. Nathaniel K. Fairbank, originally from New York City, arrived in Chicago around 1855 working as a grains salesman. A little later, he purchased a partnership in a lard-rendering plant and, within 10 years, he owned the plant. By the 1880's, his firm was producing several brands of soap, some of which—like Santa Claus—used blacks as advertising themes.

Fairbank joined hands with Armour and Morris to form a cartel designed to corner the cotton seed market; they succeeded and the American Cotton Oil Trust emerged from their manipulations, making Fairbank a millionaire. The Trust later bought Fairbank's company, retaining him as its chief executive.

Gold Dust Washing Powder was introduced during the 1880's. Its name was "so called from its gold color and exceeding fineness." It also boasted "absolute purity—not bleached by alkali." The idea of using black twins came about because of the detergent's publicity that stated, "fast colors, warranted to wash, clean and not fade." The use of blacks by Fairbank was not without precedent. Two of their products, "Golden Cottolene" and "Santa Claus," used this ethnic theme.

The product was heavily advertised and exaggerated as being a panacea. It originally sold for 25 cents in a four pound package, which had a "Beware of Imitations" warning on the top. By 1898 a bigger choice of sizes awaited the shopper, with prices starting as low as five cents.

The 1904 St. Louis Worlds Fair may be considered the highpoint of the "Gold Dust Twins" career. The Fairbank Company maintained a rather large exhibition in the fair. Atop the plain stark white columns were many statuettes of the Twins. Even more interesting was the presence of a pair of real-life Gold Dust blacks, dressed in red and blue skirts, who handed out booklets to all visitors.

The artist who actually created the "Gold Dust Twins" was E. W. Kemble, one of this country's most important and influential cartoonists. During the ten years or so that he drew them, Kemble molded the Twins' characters and personalities firmly into the national consciousness. Among his contemporaries, there are few who equal Kemble either in talent or affect on later generations of illustrators.

Edward Winsor Kemble was born in Sacramento, California in 1861. His father published a newspaper, the *Alta Californian*, but a few years later moved his family to New York where he became an inspector for the Bureau of Indian Affairs.

Though still a teenager, young Kemble was certain he wanted to become

Fig. 15. *The Gold Dust Twins.* Gold Dust products were sold in two different containers.
Courtesy, *Coll. of R. Rumohr*

an artist. While working for Western Union in New York City to earn a living, he sent many submissions to all the humor and general magazines of the day. Success was assured when some of his cartoons appeared in the September and October, 1880 issues of the important Harper's Bazaar. Soon his work was being accepted by other magazines and he could consider himself as a professional artist. He also became a political caricaturist for various New York newspapers, discovering how much he enjoyed satire.

Later Kemble hooked up with Life, and from the 1880's until the turn of the century, he devoted himself primarily to humor and satire cartooning for that publication. After this he began to turn his talents almost exclusively towards political subjects.

Somehow, between 1896 and 1905, he found time to create several comic strips for the Sunday funnies, as well as a few panels. Apart from his magazine employment, Kemble took many commissions from companies for their advertising art work. It was on such a job that he created the "Gold Dust Twins." Kemble's speciality over the years had become the American Negro and his treatment of them, while comical, was a sympathetic portrayal, quite unlike the usual treatment being given by other artists. The "Gold Dust Twins" were received with appreciation and much interest by Americans, and with Kemble's adept hand, they danced and cavorted in every home.

In addition to the many books he illustrated, such as several by Mark Twain, Kemble was also responsible for some of his own, mostly derived from his cartoons. Titles include *Kemble's Coons,** *Comical Coons* and *A Pickinniny Calendar.*

*At a "Black Americana" sale held by Richard Opfer Auctioneering October 17, 1981, "Kemble's Coons (A Collection of Southern Sketches)", R.H. Russell, N.Y. was knocked down for $90.

Like Grace Weiderseim and her Campbell Kids, the creator eventually became separated from his charges and other artists took over the job of drawing them. When radio was just coming into importance and popular use, a show titled "Gold Dust Twins" was heard over eight stations beginning in 1925 and lasting about two years. This seems to have been the last hurrah for the Twins, as they and their soap seemed to have disappeared completely by the time the Great Depression arrived, probably as victims of the times.

4
MINORITIES ON AMERICAN TRADEMARKS

Over the years, minority groups have often been the subject of trademark designers. The shiftless Black, the wild and noble Indian and the servile, pidgin-speaking Chinaman have all been featured on American trademarks. Even religious groups such as the Quakers have appeared as package trademarks. Some of these trademarks are still on the supermarket shelf while others have simply disappeared with the passage of time. Their use and popularity often reflected the manners and mores of the era in which they were born. But times have changed and these changes can normally be seen by closely examining many contemporary trademarks.

In an excellent article entitled "Racist Ephemera: The Melting Pot Reconsidered," that appeared in *American Book Collector* (Jan. - Feb. 1982), Steven Heller states:

> Until recently America's adolescence—specifically the period of mass European and Asian immigration, from the 1870's until the early 1900's—was romanticized in popular literature, music, and art. This was not unwarranted, since the ethnic diversity of the American people and the religious and political freedom they were afforded are this nation's paramount virtue. Liberty was then and remains now the personification of American ideals. Together with Uncle Sam—the embodiment of U.S. strength—Liberty was a formidable icon, an image proudly emblazoned on all manner of printed material. However, as one views the iconography of the late nineteenth and early twentieth centuries it becomes disturbingly clear that this heroic facade obscured a significant national problem.
>
> The growing pains of this young nation—exacerbated by the very melting pot policy it encouraged—were manifest in a populace uncomfortable with the new foreign inhabitants and in a government undeniably ill-equipped to deal with an alien native population and with newly freed slaves. Nowhere are this upsetting chapter of history and the emotions it conjures up revealed more profoundly than in the mass-produced popular art of the period—advertising

trade cards, posters, product labels, trademarks, sheet music, novelties, book jackets, cartoons, comic strips, book illustrations, children's literature. Through commonplace, highly visible graphic racial and ethnic stereotypes a vivid picture—sometimes scabrous, often comic—materializes of a country fraught with class, religious, and racial prejudice.

BLACKS

"I have a dream that my four children will one day live in a nation where they will not be judged by the color of their skin but by the content of their character. I have a dream today."

Dr. Martin Luther King
Washington, 1963

The racial upheavals of the late 1950's and early 1960's signaled the end to the offensive black stereotype and package trademark. Instead of the smiling uncle, big-bottomed mammy and cute little pickaninny came depictions of Blacks as a unified family with Black males contributing to society as responsible citizens. Gone were pictures of Blacks with kinky hair, huge lips and monstrous feet, a simpleton who was shiftless, unkempt and untrustworthy. Blacks were increasingly being shown as executives, athletes and happily married husbands and wives.

In 1974, Foote, Cone and Belding surveyed research in the use of Blacks on TV commercials. On the basis of existing information, the agency came to the conclusion that Black people appreciate other Blacks in commercials and that whites did not mind. The library of the Advertising Research Foundation could not come up with anything to counter that.

In 1968, a Sunday entry of the Advertising column was headlined, "The Negro Makes a Start in Commercials."

"Black America is becoming visible in America's biggest national advertising medium," it reported. "Not in a big way yet, but it is a beginning and men in high places give assurances that there will be a lot more visibility."

But the history of trademarks in the United States is tarnished by the image that the white thought was representative of the Black.

Nineteenth century (and even up into the late 1940's) trademarks usually featured Blacks as a blend of childish simplicity and foot-shuffling dependency. This image had been born in slavery and given new life in the years following Reconstruction. Trademarks and their packages closely resembled other popular depictions offered by a white society. There was a "Black Boy" brand shoe polish, a "Nigger'" brand hair pomade, a "Sambo" brand axle grease, the "Gold Dust Twins" were promoted by "Let the Gold Dust Twins

Fig. 16. *Sambo*. Sambo was a commonly used name on packages of years past. This axle grease tin measures 4½ × 3½".

Courtesy, *The James Voss Coll.*

Fig. 17. *Racist Tobacco Advertisements.* Two anti-black ads for tobacco ca. 1875–1889.

Courtesy, *National Tobacco Textile Museum, Danville, Va.*

do your work" (see Chapter III), "Kornelia Kinks" promised to brighten your day with her funny "Darky" tricks and "Lime Kiln Club" cigars featured a blatantly racist label based on a popular satire novel published in the 1880's and 90's. An article in *The Poster*, a turn-of-the-century trade magazine for outdoor advertisers, reported that Aunt Jemima and the Armour Meat Chef were the two symbols most trusted by the American housewife.

There are several popular package trademarks featuring Blacks that, although born in the nineteenth century are still in use. Their stories reflect on how history has shaped the design of many modern trademarks.

Aunt Jemima (1890)

Shrove Tuesday, Shrove Tuesday
'Fore Jack went to plow
His mother made pancakes,
She scarcely knew how.
She tossed them, she turned them,
She made them so black
With soot from the chimney
They poisoned poor Jack.

From a *Shrove Tuesday*
*Pancake Feast**

Of all the familiar trademarks, *Aunt Jemima* is one of the most appealing and expressive. Her beaming face has created a legend and given to a rather common product, pancake mix, an appealing warmth while establishing it firmly in the marketplace. She suggests abundance, pleasure and happiness, and the consumer relates these to the product in the package. Even in these "post-plantation days," Aunt Jemima still appears on the package and suggests Southern hospitality, making the Southern black woman one of the best cooks in the land. In 'fact, the product has been shown to be used by more Blacks than whites!

The first pancake mix ever made was formulated in 1888 by Chris L. Rutt, an editorial writer on the St. Joseph, Mo. *Gazette*, and a friend in the milling business, Charles G. Underwood. After countless experiments, they developed a mix of hard wheat flour, corn flour, phosphate of lime, soda and salt that, when milk was added and the batter cooked, produced pancakes which one of the first tasters later described in this way: "I ate the first perfected Aunt Jemima pancake and pronounced it good!"

A trademark and package design was soon needed to reflect the festive spirit that had always been associated with the pancake. The latter had long been associated with Lent and as a substitute for meat. In the autumn of 1889, Chris Rutt found his name and place in American package history by attending a local vaudeville house.

On the bill were two black-face comedians, Baker and Farrell. The show-stopper of their act was a jazzy, rhythmic New Orleans style cakewalk to a tune called "Aunt Jemima"**which Baker performed in the apron and red-

*The full verses of "Old Aunt Jemima" appear in: Haverly, J.H. "Haverly's Genuine Colored Minstrels Songster", Chicago, 1880, pg. 13.

**Pancakes have a long history. In England on Shrove Tuesday the church bells are rung as a signal to start making pancakes (the pancake bell). In Liberal, Kansas, a race is held on that day, with each runner carrying a pancake in a skillet. The winner must flip the pancake at least three times before crossing the finish line first.

bandanna headband of the traditional southern cook. The song started out as "Old Aunt Jemima" and was one of the most popular songs of the day done by Billy Kersands, the famous black minstrel of the 1870–1900 era. By 1877, Kersands had performed the song more than 3,000 times and had improvised three different texts for his audiences. One of the most widely sung 1875 versions used the following lines:

> *My old missus promise me,*
> *Old Aunt Jemima, oh, oh, oh, (after each line)*
> *When she died she-d set me free,*
> *She lived so long her head got bald*
> *She swore she would not die at all.*

Kersands went on to become the highest paid black minstrel of his time. His astounding popularity was partially based on his mainstay song, "Old Aunt Jemima" and "a copiousness of mouth and breadth of tongue that no white man could ever expect to rival."

Rutt immediately decided that "Aunt Jemima" was the name for the new pancake mix since it just naturally made one think of good cooking. But within a short time, Rutt and his partner ran out of money and Underwood, after registering the trademark, sold their interests to the Davis Milling Company.

R. T. Davis, the new owner of "Aunt Jemima" improved the product and set about to bring "the trademark to life." He sent requests to all his broker friends to be on the lookout for a Black woman who might exemplify southern hospitality and was also poised enough to demonstrate the product at fairs, expositions and festivals. In 1893, Davis launched a gigantic promotion at the World's Columbian Exposition in Chicago. His firm constructed

Fig. 18. *Aunt Jemima.* The famous trademark character shown on an old pancake mix box, and in a more modern version.

Courtesy, *Quaker Oats*

64

the world's largest flour barrel, inside of which displays told the story of this new pancake mix. Outside the barrel, an ex-slave named Nancy Green was hired to bring "Aunt Jemima" to life. Nancy Green had long been in the employ of a Judge Walker as a cook, nurse and, coincidentally, had made excellent pancakes. Her inherent talent and friendliness made her the ideal "Aunt Jemima" and she quickly became the hit of the fair. Over 50,000 orders were placed for "Aunt Jemima Pancake Mix" and at the end of the fair, Nancy Green was awarded a medal.

By 1910, the name was known in all 48 states and had attained such a peak of popularity that many persons attempted to infringe on the trademark rights. The name was upheld so vigorously by the courts that since the last suit in 1917, the name has not been seriously contested.

The Aunt Jemima Mills were purchased by Quaker Oats in 1925. Over a period of eighty years "Aunt Jemima" has become a national institution.

The story of "Aunt Jemima" includes two significant marketing firsts:

1. Davis was the first advertiser to bring a trademark to life. Since the moment of his inspiration, scores of advertisers have introduced living impersonations of their trademarks, particularly since the advent of animated television commercials.

2. "Aunt Jemima" has withstood the criticism of Black leaders. The "Old Auntie" offered white America warmth, devotion and love. She was an American counterpart to the European peasant, the Earth-mother. The romanticized plantation where Aunt Jemima worked served as a sanctuary where she could develop the family ties that were immune from the forces of progress. In this mythic world, she was "more dan a mudder." To modern Black leaders, she evidently does not represent slavery, degradation or servitude.* Her long history and inclusion into American folklore has seemingly superseded these characteristics. Her image still appears on the package while the symbol of her counterpart "Uncle Ben" has disappeared from the widely sold rice package.

Rastus, The Cream of Wheat Chef (1893)

"Never mind shipping us any more of your flour, but send us a car of 'Cream of Wheat'."
First orders for "Cream of Wheat" from Lamond, Corliss.

As a result of having acquired some machinery at a fire sale, three North

*Her name originated because elderly Black slaves were not referred to as Mr. or Mrs. by younger whites. They were called Aunt and Uncle in order to avoid a Mr. or Mrs. designation.

65

Dakotans, George Bull, Emery Mapes and George Clifford of Grand Forks found themselves operating a small mill in 1890. Their head miller, Thomas Amidon, was fond of taking a substance called "middlings" (i.e., farina) home to be cooked up into breakfast cereal. After a year of badgering and coaxing, he persuaded Bull, Mapes and Clifford to try selling some packaged middlings to grocery wholesalers. Mapes, who had once been a printer, secured a small supply of cartons, and dug around an old print shop he also owned, until he found an ancient woodcut of a Negro chef brandishing a skillet. With this he struck off a small supply of labels, adopted the brand name "Cream of Wheat" because they were using the best and whitest portion of the wheat, and sneaked ten cases of the new item into a carload of flour being shipped to a New York wholesaler, Lamont, Corliss and Company. Instead of the indignant complaints anticipated, the only response was a telegram for more of the same, and from that day on the product gained in popular acceptance. A few years later, while having dinner in a Chicago restaurant, Kohlsaats, Mapes noticed his waiter's infectious grin, and immediately realized that here was an effective substitute for the atrocious woodcut. The waiter was persuaded, for five dollars, to pose in a chef's cap for the famous full-face view which appeared on millions of boxes. From the day the picture was made, neither Mapes nor anyone else in the company ever saw the waiter again. Named Rastus, the smiling Cream of Wheat Chef has survived many years of change.

By 1897 the demand for "Cream of Wheat" had completely outgrown the producing capacity of the small plant at Grand Forks and the business was moved to Minneapolis. Several years later, it moved again to its own building at First Avenue North and Fifth Street. In 1928, the plant moved again to its present facility in Minneapolis. Many Negroes represented themselves as the original chef, but Mapes was in possession of certain information which made it possible for him to detect imposters.

In 1929, the stock of the Cream of Wheat Corporation was listed on the New York Stock Exchange. Cream of Wheat is today a division of Nabisco's Special Products Division.

Soul (1967)

"Soul Mellow Yellow Beer and Soul Stout Malt Liquor join James Bond 007 as the world's most wanted cans."

Beer Can Collecting (1977)

Although both Aunt Jemima and Rastus are still around, one package design, introduced in 1967, was swiftly taken off the market.

In 1967, the Maier Brewing Corporation, Los Angeles, with the Black population and market clearly in mind, introduced a new beer and malt liquor named, "Soul." "Soul Mellow Yellow Beer" was made in 12 and 16 oz. packages, while "Soul Stout Malt Liquor" was made in a 12 oz. size can. About one million cans were made. Maier had not anticipated an objection from the National Association for the Advancement of Colored People to the name of "Soul." But their protest was so strong that the brands were withdrawn after two years on the market.

For some strange reason, the brew and the background caught collector's imaginations and the cans soon commanded extraordinary prices. The cans are certainly scarce but not rare. "Soul" cans have been sold for prices up to $225 because of a false rumor that the Maier Brewery was destroyed in the race riots in the Watts section of Los Angeles that resulted in 34 deaths.

Blacks have even been used as trademarks in several foreign lands. One of the few black figures used in England as a product identification has been Robertson's "Golly." Hailing originally from Canada, he was brought to

Fig. 19. *The Robertson's Golly.*
Courtesy, *Robertson Foods Group*

England by a son of James Robertson, the founder of the confectionery business which still bears his name. Robertson junior was intrigued during a pre-First-World-War visit to the backwoods of Canada by the sight of little children playing with black rag dolls with white eyes, made from mothers' discarded black skirts and white blouses. Robertson thought that these dollies (mispronounced "gollies" by the children) would make a valuable addition to his sales force back home. Accordingly, "Golly" was adopted as a trademark by the company and given a colorful new set of clothes. It is interesting to note that "Golly" is still used by Robertson's (it is now 50 years old).

INDIANS

"A better curative agent than the youth who, after a dozen medical lectures or so is given authority as an M.D. to try his hand on anybody that comes along."
Kickapoo Almanac (1896)
speaking about the
"Noble Savage."

The glamor of the long ago and the fascination of the faraway united in the symbol of the American Indian. The Indian was a stock figure for elegaic treatment in romantic literature. He symbolized nobility, eloquence and good health. His medicines "flowed from the earth" and his face on the trademark captured the imagination of the white man. From the 1820's until about 1925, the Indian strode nobly through the American patent medicine wilderness. Hiawatha helped a hair restorative and Pocahontas blessed a bitters. Dr. Fall spent twelve years with the Creeks to discover why no Indian had ever perished of consumption. Edwin Eastman found a blood syrup among the Comanches, Texas Charley discovered a Kickapoo cure-all, and Frank Cushing pried the secret of a stomach renovator from the Zuni. There were Medoc Oil, Seminole Cough Balsam, Nez Perce Catarrah Snuff, Indian Compound of Honey, Dr. Morse's Indian Root Pills and Modox, an Indian herb beverage.

Indians were also historically used as trademarks for many tobacco products. The paintings of George Catlin (1796-1872) became the ideal on which many designers built their trademarks. "Nothing shall prevent me from becoming their historian" said Catlin of the Indians. His goals came true not only in his paintings but also in many trademarks of years ago. Notable was Catlin's Huntress Smoking Tobacco. Popular around 1900 was Captain Jack's brand cigar that featured the leader of the Medoc Wars in Northern California. Other often used cigar brands included Chief Joseph, Black Hawk and

Fig. 20. *Argo Corn Starch Maiden.*

Courtesy, *CPC International, Inc.*

Kennebec.

The symbolic figure of the Indian on the trademark is still used today. Most famous are Argo brand Corn Starch*, Best Food's Mazola*, Indian-head brand Yellow Corn Meal and Land O'Lakes brand butter and margarine. They reflect the long association of the Indian with corn, the earth and wholesomeness.

In *The White Man's Indian*, Robert F. Berkhofer discusses the birth of the noble savage and the evil heathen myths, showing their roots in early woodblock prints which were widely distributed in eighteenth-century England and France. This image was perpetuated throughout the Continent by the misguided romanticism and idealism of the philosophers, who saw the Indian as the embodiment of the New World—a naif on the one hand and a fearless hunter on the other. And so the white man's Indian became the graphic symbol of the new frontier, appearing on flags, banners and emblems. Indians were used to sell tobacco, beer, medicines—and later— automobiles, vegetables, fruits and clothing.

*Argo brand cornstarch is a product of Best Foods, a div. of CPC International, Inc. The Indian Maid trademark was devised and first used in 1913 by Corn Products Refining Co. It is registered as U.S. trademark numbers 96,572 dated April 21, 1914 and 596,170 dated October 5, 1954; the trademark has been modified slightly over the years.

The Indian "Mazola" Girl (1980)

Mazola brand margarine currently uses an American Indian spokeswoman to play up the natural corn goodness of its ingredients. Selected for the job was Tenaya, a contemporary full-blooded Apache born in Las Cruces, New Mexico.

Tenaya is used in Mazola's "Goodness from Maize" strategy on TV quite successfully. Each commercial in the campaign closes with Tenaya saying "Remember Mazola margarine. It gets its goodness from maize." The response from the American Indian community has been positive because the use of the Indian as the central character has been both dignified and constructive.

Best Foods' use of an Indian spokeswoman for Mazola is a rarity on the talent side. Perhaps it will become a future trend?

CHINESE

Our distant brothers, the Chinese,
Long fam'd for their refreshing Teas,
Produce a Cream, so rich and full,
That clothes with hair the baldest skull.
S.C. Gaz, (Nov. 21, 1743)

The oriental wisdom of the Chinese was captured on the many 19th century nostrums bearing such names as Dr. Lin's Celestial Balm of China, Dr. Drake's Canton Chinese Hair Cream and Carey's Chinese Catarrah Cure. The trademark usually caught the strangeness of it all! Dr. Lin presented an exquisite engraving of a Chinese sage sitting in an elaborate chair; one servant held a parasol over his worthy head while another brought a bottle of the balm. Dr. Drake also pictured an oriental scene. Yet, even though the Westerner thought highly of Chinese wisdom, a definite prejudice existed. In the 1870's, the Chinese became the subject of racist cigar labels in reaction to their growing importance in California and New York industries, a fact bitterly resented in most cigar-making centers. Chinese were also depicted as laundry experts and their faces adorned many laundry starches, washboards and clothespin packages.

The vision of the Chinese that many Europeans maintained was exotic and mysterious. Most popular prints portrayed these people as beautifully clad lords whose pastime was opium smoking. The American conception was based firmly on the appearance of the peasant who immigrated to the West Coast to work on the railroad. Using the traditional hair braid—called a pigtail or queue—as a focus, the cartoonist transformed the coolie into an anthropomorphized rat. An 1888 package of rat poison shows a Chinese man about to eat a rat!

The 20th century has seen the disappearance of the negative Chinese stereotype and symbolic Chinese trademarks are usually seen only on ethnic foods and teas. After years of Charlie Chan, "Godzilla" and kung fu roles—with Macy's and Wise potato chips still using Chan types in ads—Orientals are now being considered for more dignified roles.

QUAKERS

"Quaker was the first to make a national food label significant, first to market a breakfast cereal nationally, first to promote a food by national advertising, first to register a cereal trademark."
Brands, Trademarks and
Good Will (1967) p. 8

In 1650, George Fox started a new religious sect calling themselves "Friends." The group soon became known as "Quakers" because of a judge who, in derision when Fox bade him "tremble at the word of the Lord," called him a "quaker."

The sect quickly became associated with purity, good sense, sterling honesty, solidity, strength and manliness. The group caught the fancy of some patent medicine concerns who sent out representatives known in the show business and carnival world as "Quaker doctors." These merry gentlemen, more thespians than doctors, were dressed somewhat in the style of Elbert Hubbard. They "thee'd" and "thou'd" around the tent, and called the customers "Friend." The quaker gimmick caught the public fancy and many patent medicines appeared bearing Quaker names. Dr. Flint's Quaker Bitters was one of the most famous preparations having a Quaker name.

In later years one firm took the Quaker symbol and made it known worldwide—*The Quaker Oats Company.*

Quaker Oats (1877)

"Those who eat Quaker Oats have less desire for meat, and they will always tell you that they feel better."
Quaker Oats Statement (1890)

In 1877, the Quaker Mill Company was organized in Ravenna, Ohio by Henry Parsons Crowell, Henry Seymour and William Heston. Henry Seymour, searching an encyclopedia for a virtuous identity that would instill buyer confidence, saw in the article on the Quaker sect exactly the connotation he desired for his steel-cut oats. Possibly his eye was on the large Quaker population in nearby Ohio towns and villages. The Quaker symbol was given commercial form in 1877 when the Quaker Mill Company registered as a trademark the "figure of a man in Quaker garb," to which in 1895 the name "Quaker" was added in another registry. The 1877 filing was America's first registered trademark for a breakfast cereal.

William Heston also lays claim to the distinction of having chosen the Quaker trademark. He was of Quaker descent, which may have motivated the trademark, but this is doubtful. Heston's story is that while walking through the streets of Cincinnati one day, he saw a picture of William Penn, clothed in Quaker garb. He immediately decided that "Quaker" was a name that would carry connotations of quality and would make an ideal trademark.

The "Quaker Man" was soon a tremendous success, even though it inspired costly law suits, both here and abroad, and was once even defended against the Society of Friends who petitioned Congress, unsuccessfully, to bar trademarks with any religious connotations.

Much of the success of Quaker Oats is credited to Henry Crowell. He was one of the first men in American industry to visualize the unlimited advantages of selling a packaged product. He pioneered the package because his

Fig. 21. *The Quaker Man.*
Courtesy, *Werbin and Morrill, Inc.*

box was essentially a sales message and recipe rather than merely something to hold the product. The folding carton, used by Crowell for Quaker Oats, was scarcely perfected at the time. Its patent had been in effect less than ten years!

The distinction of the Crowell carton was the prominent display of a printed trademark in impressive colors and the printing of sales and recipe information. This was possible because the unfolded carton lay flat and could be passsed through the impression rollers of a printing press. Crowell proclaimed the man in "Quaker garb" and offered premiums to consumers who would cut out the Quaker figure and mail it to him, thus further impressing the trademark upon them.

By 1893, the Quaker symbol has undergone subtle changes. Printing of the trademark in color inspired a redesign. The gaunt and austere Quaker gave way to a genial, fat-bellied one, more ostentatious than any Friend would permit—with a red vest under his blue tailored coat and golden buckles on his patent leather shoes. In this role he was a familiar resident of the American scene for many years. He appeared personally at fairs and exhibitions. International interest was even aroused when a gigantic likeness of the "Quaker Man" was placed on the White Cliffs of Dover. It took an act of Parliament to have the sign removed.

Other religious groups have appeared as trademarks—the Shakers, Dukhoboretsi and even the Millerites. But only the "Quaker Man" has resisted the ravages of time.

5

COLAS, DR PEPPER, ROOT BEER AND THE "UN-COLA"

"We earnestly believe that at some future date the cola nut, when becoming better known, may be found a not to be despised competitor of tea and coffee."

New Idea (March, 1884)

When scientist Joseph Priestly devised a way to put carbon dioxide into water in 1772, soda water was born. Early carbonated beverages were sealed with porcelain stoppers which, when pushed in, released the carbon dioxide in the bottle with a "pop." Thus, in the 1880's, the name "soda pop" was born. It was also during the same era that many of the famous soft drinks were first introduced to the American public.

Coca-Cola

"Delicious and Refreshing" (1886)
"The Pause that Refreshes" (1929)
"Things Go Better With Coke" (1963)
Coca-Cola Slogans

Coca-Cola, one of the world's best known trademarks, was originated by an ex-Confederate soldier named John Styth Pemberton of Wheeler's Cavalry C.S.A., known to his friends as Major and as Doctor. When the Civil War ended, he went into the drug business in Atlanta, at which he was not a conspicuous success. His problem was that he was constantly experimenting, so after producing several proprietaries, he decided to concentrate all his efforts on a soft drink. After considerable trial and error, he came up with a formula

74

on May 8, 1886, that satisfied him. He mixed the first batch of the new formula in a three-legged brass pot over a wood fire in the back yard of an antebellum red brick house. He had achieved the blend of flavors that he had long sought and now needed to name the product. His friend and bookkeeper, Frank M. Robinson, came up with the answer—an alliterative compounding of two of the many ingredients of the new drink—"coca" (the dried leaves of a South American shrub), and "cola" (an extract of the kola nut). He firmly believed that "the two C's would look well in advertising." Robinson also wrote the name in flowing Spencerian script, much as it appears today. On January 31, 1893, Coca-Cola became the first cola beverage ever registered in the Patent Office.*

Coca-Cola was originally created in syrup form to be used in Atlanta soda fountains, and full rights to the product were acquired in 1888 by another young Atlanta druggist, Asa G. Chandler for $2,300. Dr. Pemberton had died the year before and Chandler decided to devote full time to Coca-Cola and in 1892 organized the Coca-Cola company.

The early 5¢ Coke was nonalcoholic, but it did use *ERTHROZYLON COCA* plants in its original formula. The untreated leaves of this plant contain small amounts of cocaine, which, as used in the drink, provided such a miniscule amount of the drug that at least eight quarts would have to have been consumed at one sitting in order to produce delirium tremens. In July

Fig. 22. *The Famous "Coke" Bottle.* An American symbol.

Courtesy, *The Coca-Cola Company*

*The name Coca-Cola had been used in the marketplace since 1886.

1894   1899–1902   1900 ———— 1916   1915

Fig. 23. *Chronology of the Glass Package for Coca-Cola.*

Courtesy, *The Coca-Cola Company*

1923   1937   1957   1961   1975

COLAS, DR PEPPER, ROOT BEER, THE "UNCOLA"

1884, Freud presented his famous "Coca" paper, outlining the evils of the drug. By 1906, the Pure Food and Drug Act, limiting the use of opiates in food products, was passed by Congress. Anticipating the passage of this bill, the Coca-Cola Company had already treated its leaves so that no trace of the drug could be found in their formula by government agents. In spite of this, the Coca-Cola "cocaine" legend persisted up into the 1930's.

In 1892, high-speed bottling machinery began to evolve and the infancy of the bottled drink industry was at hand. In 1894, an enterprising dealer began to bottle a mixture of the syrup and carbonated water for sale outside the Atlanta area. Five years later, Chandler sold exclusive rights to bottle and sell Coca-Cola in most of the United States to Benjamin Thomas and Joseph Whitehead. The contract was to bottle the drink only—not to manufacture the syrup from which Coca-Cola was prepared.* The concept of locally owned and operated bottling plants was now established, and Chandler eventually sold the company in 1919 to Ernest Woodruff, whose son Robert began to market the drink throughout the world. It is now sold in more than 135 countries, at the rate of 233 million drinks daily.

The name Coke first appeared on labels in 1941, and was officially registered in 1945. The distinctive curved and fluted Coca-Cola bottle became a registered trademark in 1960, an honor accorded to only a handful of other packages. Designer Raymond Loewy, who had no connection with the bottle's design, called the bottle, "the most perfectly designed package in use today."

Pepsi-Cola

Pepsi-Cola hits the spot
Twelve full ounces, that's a lot
Twice as much for a nickel, too
Pepsi-Cola is the drink for you.
Pepsi-Cola Company
(1940) - Jingles

In the summer of 1898, Caleb Bradham, a young New Bern, North Carolina pharmacist, began to experiment with cola beans to formulate a new soft drink to sell at his drug store's fountain. He concocted a blend of sugar, vanilla, rare oils, spices and the cola nut, among other ingredients. His cronies hailed it as excellent, and promptly named it "Brad's Drink" in his

---

*The Coca-Cola company manufactures and sells a concentrated syrup under the trademark Coca-Cola to its licensed bottlers who, under the license, are permitted to combine the syrup with carbonated water according to specifications laid down by The Coca-Cola company and to sell the resultant beverage under the trademark, Coca-Cola.

honor. But by August 28, 1898, young Bradham himself had given it the name "Pepsi-Cola."

Bradham's first step was to register Pepsi-Cola as his trademark at the Patent Office in Washington. The application was filed September 23, 1902, and is the earliest dated document in Pepsi-Cola history. In it Bradham stated, "This mark has been continuously used in my business since August 1, 1901." The application was accepted by the Patent Office and the mark duly registered on June 16, 1903. While awaiting final registration by the Patent Office, Bradham, on April 9, 1903, registered his trademark "Pepsi-Cola" in the office of the Secretary of State of North Carolina, and in that registration gave as the date of earliest use, not August 1, 1901, but August 28, 1898.

Later, in 1906, he registered "Pepsi-Cola" a second time in the Patent Office, and in that second registration gave as the date of earliest use, not August 1, 1901, or August 28, 1898, but February 15, 1896; but in doing that he was referring not to a "Pepsi-Cola" date but to a "Pep-Kola" date. For at this time there was already on the market, with trademark registration since February 15, 1896, a drink named Pep-Kola; and on March 21, 1903, Bradham had purchased that trademark and registered it in his own name in the Patent Office, continuing always thereafter to own it. Having thus acquired ownership of the the Pep-Kola mark, Bradham seems to have felt that his name in some way "derived" from it, for in his 1906 registration he stated: "This trademark has been continuously used in my business, and those from whom title is derived, since February 15, 1896."

But that date, February 15, 1896, was the Pep-Kola date, the date of its registration in the Patent Office. The earliest date of Pepsi-Cola use, as shown from Bradham's North Carolina registration, was August 28, 1898. By 1904, Bradham was bottling his new drink, and a year later, the first two franchises were operating in Charlotte and Durham, North Carolina.

Bottling carbonated beverages was a hazardous adventure in the early days. A pedal pump was used for filling and a wire stopper for crowning, while a mask over the operator's face guarded him against exploding bottles. In fact, bottles, which were cleaned with lead shot, were not even standard, with beer bottles often doing double duty for soft drinks. Frequently, the bottler made deliveries himself by horse and wagon.

In 1907, as Pepsi-Cola Company grew, there were 40 franchises primarily in the Carolinas and Virginia, and one as far west as Arizona, still five years away from statehood.

By World War I, 300 bottlers were operating in 24 states. But during the war years, the price of sugar, vital in the manufacture of the Pepsi-Cola syrup sold to bottlers, was frozen. Restrictions were lifted at the end of the war and

1898 – 1905

1906 – 1936

1937 – 1950

1951 – Present

1962 – 1969

1970 – Present

Fig. 24. *Various Pepsi-Cola Trademarks.*
Courtesy, *Pepsi Co., Inc. Copyright and Trademark owner*

the price of sugar shot up. Bradham bought heavily as a hedge against even higher prices, but he guessed wrong. By the end of 1920, sugar prices had plummeted.

Both company and bottlers were hard hit and money was impossible to raise. For the next 15 years, Pepsi-Cola's fortunes waned. Constantly reorganized and refinanced, Pepsi-Cola Company at one point in the early 1930's had only two bottlers left in the entire United States.

But help was on the way. Loft, Inc., a northern chain of candy stores, had been looking for a new soft drink to add to its fountain trade. So in 1931, Loft acquired 80 percent of a newly formed Pepsi-Cola Company and began a vast expansion program to provide the badly needed volume and distribution.

Although court battles for control of the Company still lay ahead, Pepsi-Cola began to move out of its dark ages in 1934 by selling 12-ounces of its drink for the same nickel that customers were accustomed to paying for six-and-a-half ounces. Later, to promote this bargain, the world's first radio advertising jingle was aired:

> *Pepsi-Cola hits the spot.*
> *Twelve full ounces,*
> *That's a lot.*
> *Twice as much for a nickel, too,*
> *Pepsi-Cola is the drink for you.*

It became one of the most memorable and effective slogans in the history of advertising and Pepsi-Cola Company.

Almost overnight Pepsi-Cola sales soared. Bargain-seeking depression-worn America responded to "Twice as much for a nickel." Dozens of other soft-drink manufacturers hurriedly switched to 12-ounce bottles, but none enjoyed Pepsi-Cola's success.

The Company entered a new era. "Twice as much for a nickel" was to give way to slogans geared to a time of growing prosperity: "Be Sociable, Have a Pepsi"; "The Light Refreshment"; and, in the 1960's, with young people targeted as the key consumers, "Now it's Pepsi for Those Who Think Young"; and "Come Alive, You're in the Pepsi Generation," a slogan that was to add a new phrase to the language. "Taste that Beats the Others Cold," "You've Got a Lot to Live, Pepsi's Got a Lot to Give," and Diet Pepsi's Girlwatchers campaign became national popular favorites. In 1974, "Join the Pepsi People, Feelin' Free" continued Pepsi-Cola's tradition of great advertising.

Dr Pepper*

Scientists tell us that all space is an ocean of ether in which our solar system swims, and that all life, animal and vegetable, is derived from the sun's energy transmitted to our planet by the ether. Plant life organizes this energy for us in nature's laboratory.

As animals, we then partake of nature's bountiful store and the sun's energy. Certain fruits, nuts and sugar can represent this energy and vitality best.

We have found this great natural law, and we combine these substances with distilled water. The name of our combination is Dr. Pepper. . . . 'Liquid Sunshine'.

R. S. Lazenby (1913)

"King of Beverages" (1886)
"Drink a Bite to Eat at 10, 2 and 4 o'clock" (1926)
"Be a Pepper" (1977)

Dr Pepper Slogans

Dr Pepper's origin in 1885 is as unique as its flavor, often described as more distinctive and different than any other carbonated soft drink in America.

It all began with a young pharmacist, Wade Morrison, working at a drug store in Rural Retreat, Virginia which was owned by a doctor by the name of Pepper. Dr. Pepper had an attractive teenage daughter who caught the eye of young Morrison and soon a budding romance developed. The doctor, feeling the romance was premature, discouraged the affair.

Morrison decided to "go West" as many other young men were doing. He traveled to Texas where he landed a job as a pharmacist working for the Tobin Drug Store in Austin, Texas. Shortly after, the owners opened another drug store in Round Rock, Texas.

Morrison was sent to Round Rock to work in the new store. At the time he was working at the Tobin Drug in Round Rock, Sam Bass and his notorious outlaw band attempted to hold up the bank there and young Morrison witnessed the historic episode that followed. Texas Rangers had been forewarned of the planned robbery and were laying in ambush. The holdup was thwarted

*In May, 1950, the period after Dr was dropped by the Dr Pepper Company to improve the readability of the logo. New designs were introduced in 1957 and 1961, and the current style debuted in 1971, but none included the period.

and Bass, along with several of his band, was killed.

Soon afterward Morrison moved to Waco, Texas to work in a drug store owned by John W. Castles. It wasn't long before he became a partner with Castles and the store became known as Castles & Morrison Drugs.

A year later Morrison purchased the store from Castles and changed its name to Morrison's Old Corner Drug.

Joining Morrison, also working as a pharmacist, was a young graduate of the University of Texas Medical School, Charles C. Alderton. A native of Brooklyn, N.Y., he had received his early schooling in Stowmarket, England. Typical of his English ancestry, Alderton was an inventive chap. Even though he had an M.D. degree, he elected to work as a pharmacist. His medical expertise was soon well known in the area.

Alderton was fascinated by the store's soda fountain and enjoyed "experimenting" by mixing the various fruit flavors. He had noted that fountain patrons often were undecided as to what they would order from the wide variety of flavors including grape, strawberry, cherry, lemon, sarsaparilla and others. This led him to put together a combination of some of these, one of which turned out to be particularly palatable.

Alderton began offering his new drink combination to the fountain patrons. He had tried it out on Morrison, the proprietor, who found it to his

Fig. 25. *Dr Pepper Bottle.* Seven oz. bottle; vintage early 1900.
Courtesy, *Dr Pepper Company*

liking. The new drink was indeed unusual and different and customers enjoyed it. They began calling for it and its popularity gained rapidly.

Morrison had not forgotten his earlier infatuation with the Virginia doctor's daughter and spoke often about it to his friends. At this point someone brought up the question of a name for the new drink they were serving. One thing led to another and finally it was suggested they name the drink after the Virginia doctor, the idea being that it might curry favor for Morrison.

Out of this unique situation Dr Pepper acquired its name—stemming from Morrison's youthful romance with the daughter of the Virginia doctor.

Conjecture, or perhaps romanticism, had Morrison returning to Rural Retreat, Virginia, where he supposedly married the doctor's daughter, but this was only fancy. While working in Round Rock, Morrison had met Carrie Jeffress, whom he later married, thus eliminating an otherwise romantic ending to his Virginia love affair.

The Dr Pepper drink continued to grow in favor and many were calling for it regularly at the Old Corner Drug fountain. Other drug store proprietors in Waco, hearing of the new drink and its growing popularity, approached Morrison about buying some of the flavoring syrup. He and Alderton began mixing up quantities for sale to the other stores. Demand increased rapidly as other fountain patrons began enjoying the drink.

Fig. 26. *Dr Pepper Bottle with Paper Label,* commonly known today among collectors as the "Thief Bottle." So far as is known Dr Pepper was the only product to appear in such a bottle. Its vintage is from 1908–1912.

Courtesy, *Dr Pepper Company*

Fig. 27. *Reverse Side of "Thief Bottle"* with inscription, "We pay for evidence convicting thieves for refilling our bottles." The A.M. & B. Company was the Artesian Bottling & Mfg. Co., forerunner of Dr Pepper Company and the original bottler of Dr Pepper.

Courtesy, *Dr Pepper Company*

Soon Morrison was faced with a problem. He could no longer produce enough of the syrup in his drug store. At this point, another figure entered the picture. R. S. Lazenby, a young Waco beverage chemist, was a frequent customer of the Old Corner Drug. He had tasted their new fountain drink and was impressed like all the others. Lazenby, only two years earlier, had opened his Circle "A" Ginger Ale Bottling Works within a block or so from the Old Corner Drug.

Morrison went to see Lazenby about producing the Dr Pepper flavoring syrup in his bottling plant. It took little persuasion to work out an arrangement since Lazenby liked the drink and was aware of its growing popularity. As a result of this meeting, Lazenby began making the Dr Pepper syrup in his plant. He became further interested in its possibilities and, together with Morrison, they considered bottling the drink. In 1885, Dr Pepper was first used by the Circle "A" Ginger Ale Company for their initial trials with the soft drink.

Before this was done, however, Lazenby conducted considerable research on the product, making a number of refinements in its quality and flavor. Since Alderton, the originator, had no plans for the drink, he willingly agreed that Morrison and Lazenby pursue their idea for bottling Dr Pepper. It was then that Morrison and Lazenby formed the Artesian Mfg. & Bottling Works, which would then become the original company to bottle Dr Pepper.

From that point, Dr Pepper went on to become one of the leading soft drinks on the American market. It has grown to the fourth largest-selling brand in America with complete domestic distribution and has expanded its availability into Canada, Japan, Ireland, Malta, Saudi Arabia and a number of other international markets.

More than 500 independent franchised bottling companies are now producing and marketing Dr Pepper. The product enjoys several distinctions. It is an original flavor, neither cola, root beer nor any single flavor.

The Company has capitalized on this unique and distinct flavor of Dr Pepper. It is the only carbonated soft drink that has experienced success served as a hot beverage.

As interesting as Dr Pepper's early beginning is its sales and earnings growth record. The formative years didn't actually begin until the early twenties after the company moved its base of operations from Waco, Texas to Dallas. This was the beginning of the mushroom period for Dr Pepper when its availability was to spread beyond the Southwest.

By 1930 net sales had reached $1,531,719.46 and earnings $387,329.46. In the ten-year period following sales more than tripled to $3,399,792 and earnings climbed to $731,187.41. This same growth rate continued and by

1970 annual net sales hit $61,028,665 and earnings were $5,733,917. In the eight years following, net sales escalated to $271,008,000 and earnings reached $23,565,000.

There are two things remarkable about Dr Pepper. It grew out of an original creation by a young pharmacist in Waco, Texas, and nearly 100 years hence, it is still recognized for its original flavor. Many attempts have been made to copy the Dr Pepper flavor, none successful.

Another interesting fact about Dr Pepper is its place of origin, not out of an inventor's laboratory nor as a result of extensive research. In fact, it was more by happenstance that young Charles Alderton hit upon this unique drink at the Old Corner Drug in Waco, Texas in 1885.

Hires Root Beer

"Hires to You!"
"Catch a Draft"
Hires Slogans

While C. E. Hires, a Philadelphia pharmacist was honeymooning in New Jersey, he was served an herb tea. He enjoyed the flavor so much that upon returning to his drugstore in Philadelphia, he created a drink from root, bark and berries, which he named Hires Herb Tea. A friend, then the president of Columbia University, suggested the name be made congenial to the beer-drinking habits of the Philadelphia public, so the product was renamed Hires Root Beer. A merchandising genius, Hires gave out free samples, took newspaper ads and created trade cards with a color picture on one side and an ad on the other. The cards were given free to customers, who began to collect them much as baseball cards were collected later. Sales soared and Hires became an integral part of the American scene.

7 - Up

"7-Up the Uncola" *(1976)*
"America's Turning 7-Up" *(1978)*
7-Up Slogans

C. L. Grigg's Howdy Company wanted to market a drink with a lemon-lime flavor. After 11 attempts, "Bib-Label Lithiated Lemon-Lime Soda" was introduced—two weeks before the stock market crash in 1929. The 7-Up trademark had been registered the year before (August 7, 1928) and was given to the new product so as to take advantage of the simpler name.

Soft drink trademarks and graphics have contributed greatly to American business. Products such as Dad's Root Beer, Canada Dry Pale Ginger Ale, Stewarts Root Beer and many others have all reflected the good design and sharp graphics so necessary for a successful product.

Fig. 28. *The 7-Up Trademark.* The history of the mark and its current use on various bottles.

Courtesy, *7-Up Co.*

86

6

THE TRADEMARK
MENAGERIE

*"Almost all American cars have virile, phallic, sexy
names. Ford has the Mustang, Maverick, Cougar.
General Motors has a Panther, Wildcat, Impala,
Firebird. Even pipe tobacco has names such as
Lionhead, Barking Dog, Kingbee, Bull Durham."**
Packaging: The Sixth Sense?
Ernest Dichter, Cahners
Books (1975)

After the Civil War ended and the increasing use of packaged products
by consumers became noticeable, the then fledgling advertising industry urgently needed an entirely new range of symbols to identify its products. In an
unsophisticated age with widespread illiteracy, it was only natural that animals, birds and even fish were used to captivate the minds and tease the
imagination of the consumer. The animals would evoke solid and accessible
images. Soon, these trademarks rapidly grew into a whole new pantheon of
domestic deities. There were cuddlesome kittens, raging bulls, nobly fierce
lions, downy chicks and barking dogs (see Table 6.2). Many products and
services still retain their original animal trademark. By this unbroken conti-
nuity, they have given a certain degree of warmness and familiarity to their
products. Their appeal is often nostalgic and projects considerable charm to
the product. (Indeed, Dr. Ernest Dichter, the famed motivational researcher,
has found that more than 78 percent of the space on packaging is devoted to
auxiliary symbols (colors, objects, people). The combination, he said, is designed to convey "happiness, sadness, love, safety and other emotions sub-
liminally.") But to the complex multifaceted corporation, animal symbols
have become rather passé. Walter P. Margulies in *Advertising Age*, (Nov. 7,

*Note Table 6.1

87

1977) says, "With important exceptions, those that still serve tend to be survivors of a different period in the history of business. Their continued presence is usually a function of tradition and high recognition, rather than of specific marketing or identity planning."

TABLE 6.1

CAR LETTER SYMBOLS

Manufacturer	Letter	Car
General Motors	A	Chevrolet Celebrity Pontiac 6000 Oldsmobile Ciera Buick Century
	X	Chevrolet Citation Pontiac Phoenix Oldsmobile Omega Buick Skylark
	F	Chevrolet Camaro Pontiac Firebird
	J	Chevrolet Cavalier Pontiac J2000 Cadillac Cimarron
	K	Cadillac Seville
	B	Chevrolet Impala Chevrolet Caprice Classic Oldsmobile Delta 88 Buick LeSabre
	E	Oldsmobile Toronado Buick Riviera Cadillac El Dorado
	T	Chevrolet Chevette Pontiac T1000
Chrysler	K	Plymouth Aries Dodge Reliant

*In the industry's earliest days, Ford used letters, the "T" and "A", but letters gave way to names intended to suggest things like *speed* (Skylark, Phantom, Bonneville) or *wealth* (Newport, LeBaron, El Dorado). In recent years, the names have been retired, but letters have been used often to describe bodies shared by more than one division in a company.

Fig. 29. *Peek Freans Teddy Bear Biscuits.* An early use of the teddy bear as a product trademark. Courtesy, *Walter Landor Associates Museum of Packaging Antiquities*

TABLE 6.2

ANIMALS AS CIGAR BRANDS

Animal	Brand
Horse	Harvester, Vanko, Alcazar, Old Dan, Old Coon and Dobbin
Elephant	White Elephant
Fish	Shad
Bird	Blue Jay, Red Bird, Egret, Golden Oriole, Pheasant, Two Homers, Eagle, Swan, White Owl, Black Hawk, Chicks, War Eagle
Lion	White Lion

Fig. 30. *A Rabbit.* Animal branded cigar labels. Courtesy, *Coll. of Tony Hyman*

Fig. 31. *Three Jackasses.* Another animal brand cigar label. Courtesy, *Coll. of Tony Hyman*

89

HORSE

The symbol of the horse, particularly the white horse, has always had a romantic and noble association. A white horse has always been a symbol of purity and high ideals and an emblem of power and victory. The horse gods went forth to war on snow white horses; the Valkyrie rode white horses; and the horses of many generals—from the Saxons Hengist and Horsa to Napoleon and Gen. Robert E. Lee's Traveller—were white.

In Scotland, the best whisky was often served in the nation's many inns and taverns. Out of this drinking habit came the name of one of the most famous Scotch whiskies—White Horse.

White Horse Distillers Ltd. is one of the big five Companies which dominate the Scotch Whisky industry today. The Company holds the Royal Warrant, employs over 800 people and blends, bottles and stores millions of gallons of whisky which are distributed throughout the world and enjoyed by consumers in 180 countries.

It was on the Island of Islay that the WHITE HORSE story really began.* The business activities of the predecessors of White Horse Distillers can be dated back to 1742 when a man by the name of Johnston operated ten small "bothies"—little one-room huts in which illicit stills produced "uisge-beatha", Gaelic for whisky—the water of life.

These were the great days of smuggling, and since Islay was one of the principal sources of the water of life, a most prosperous trade was carried on from there. In 1801 all these buildings were converted into a legal distillery, named Lagavulin, by a William Graham and his son Alexander, and in 1845 James Logan Mackie joined them in partnership. Shortly afterwards Peter Jeffrey Mackie, a nephew of Logan Mackie, trained there as a distiller, and later, when his uncle retired, took over the company. The single malt whisky produced there ranked high in fame, even then.

From 1860, HM Customs and Excise permitted the blending of whiskies from the different distilleries. The technique of blending—balancing the full bodied malt whiskies of the Highlands against the lighter Lowland malts and grains—made possible the emergence of distinctive brands, which were uniform in character from year to year, milder than the strongly flavoured malt whiskies and which therefore appealed to a larger public.

The growth of a wider market began with the Franco-Prussian war, which created boom conditions in the iron and coal industry of Southern Scotland. So, throughout the seventies, miners and steelworkers enjoyed high wages and sales of blended whisky substantially increased.

*The name White Horse was officially registered in 1891.

90

Fig. 32. *The Famous White Horse Brand Scotch.*
Courtesy, *White Horse Distillers, Ltd.*

The swing of public taste continued to spread and one by one the famous blends were introduced. In the late 1880's Mackies' White Horse Cellar Scotch Whisky was added to the growing list of high quality blended whiskies.

The Mackies were an old Stirlingshire family who had owned property in Edinburgh since 1650. Near the family home was one of the most famous of all ancient inns—the White Horse Inn in the Canongate. The Inn had always attracted famous literary and theatrical people; Dr. Johnson and Samuel Foote were frequent visitors. Earlier, the White Horse Inn had been a favorite rendezvous for Prince Charles Edward's cavaliers. It was indeed rich in Highland history and atmosphere.

All Edinburgh knew the White Horse Cellar as the starting place for the London stage coach, which departed on Mondays and Fridays at five in the morning. The journey was advertised as taking eight days (if God permits) and the intrepid travelers were allowed 14 lbs of luggage with a charge of 12 cents a pound for excess luggage. The legendary background and the rich past of the White Horse Cellar inspired Peter Mackie to choose the name "White Horse" for his whisky. Today, the WHITE HORSE label still shows this historic link with the old White Horse Cellar with the original announcement, dated 1754, and the stage coach pulled by a team of horses.

Under the leadership of Peter Mackie, WHITE HORSE SCOTCH WHISKY achieved international status. He traveled the world to establish the brand as a market leader in many countries overseas. At home he also became prominent in politics, sport and public works, and in 1920 was created a Baronet.

Through his efforts and those of the other pioneers of the Company, WHITE HORSE achieved a truly international distribution, establishing great prestige, both for itself and for the Scotch Whisky industry as a whole, in the world's major markets. The reputation of the brand grew, both from the label and from the energy and drive of the executives, whose job it was to travel the world dealing with the Company's local distributors.

These distributors were themselves highly respected companies in their own countries and their prestige in local markets did much to help WHITE HORSE attain the status of market leader.

In 1924, the year of Sir Peter Mackie's death, the Company took its present title. Two years later White Horse introduced the screw cap and almost doubled its turnover on the home market in six months. Then in 1927, WHITE HORSE became part of the Distillers Company Limited.

The horse symbol has also been used on clothes (Levi Strauss & Co.'s Two Horse brand overalls and the more recent Jordache jeans), automotive products (Socony's Flying Red Horse) and for automobiles (Mustang). It has not been used for food products, possibly because of its poor connotation with edible products.

Fig. 33. *Another Scotch Bearing the White Horse.*
Courtesy, *White Horse Distillers, Ltd.*

LION

Metro-Goldwyn-Mayer's (MGM) Leo, its trademark lion, is one of the most widely known animal trademarks.

Leo owes its theatrical fame to the founder of MGM—Samuel Goldwyn, a Polish immigrant. When Goldwyn launched the Goldwyn Company, he hired a New York advertising agency to promote both the company and its motion pictures. A recent Columbia graduate, Howard Dietz, was given the job of dreaming up a suitable trademark. Dietz was still very much attached to his alma mater and one Saturday in 1916 attended a Columbia football game. As the cheer leaders led the students in the rousing Columbia song, "Roar, Lion, Roar", the team mascot, Leo, bounded onto the field. Inspired by the drama of the occasion, Dietz quickly selected the lion as Goldwyn's trademark.

Soon Leo appeared on the screen with a motto in Latin "Ars Gratia Artis"—"Art is Beholden to the Artists"—giving him both distinction and character. As the Goldwyn Company grew and eventually became the now familiar MGM, Leo retained his enviable position. One recurring problem was that every time an MGM official heard about a new lion in town, an order was issued for his photograph and the new lion was substituted for the old one. In the space of a decade, a pile of "official" Leo's began to pile up. To settle all the confusion, MGM decided to issue a heart-rendering tale that the real Leo was returned to Africa and set free in the jungle. To the dismay of the MGM publicity people, the studio was soon swamped with letters from animal lovers all over the world. After all, a lion reared in captivity would have a terrible time trying to survive in the jungle. MGM's press agents quickly revised the story to say that the real Leo would not be sent to Africa after all; he would be retired and spend his days in a spacious domestic zoo. Actually no one at MGM knew which Leo the public was talking about nor why there was all this fuss about a made-up trademark.

DOG

The image of the dog has been featured on scores of American products, from the bull dog on Bull Dog brand suspenders to the two little Scotch terriers on the label of Black and White brand Scotch. But perhaps three of the most famous dog trademarks are Nipper, the Victor talking machine dog, the greyhound of the Greyhound Bus Company and Tige, Buster Brown's Boston bulldog.

93

Fig. 34. *Bulldog Brand Sauces.*
Courtesy, *Bull-Dog Sauce Co., Ltd.*

RCA Victor's Nipper

Nipper was an obese fox terrier whose owner died somewhere around 1895. Adopted by a London artist named Francis Barraud, he was the subject of a sentimental Victorian painting that Barraud titled, "His Master's Voice." Nipper had been seen peering intently into an early gramophone and Barraud captured the pose magnificently in oil.

The original painting depicted Nipper listening to his master's voice (Barraud's recently deceased brother) on a cylinder machine, but having failed to sell the picture to a phonograph manufacturer, he was persuaded by the Gramophone Company (now EMI) to paint out the phonograph and substitute a gramophone.*

The first gramophone records with circular paper title label were devised by Eldridge Johnson and issued by the Consolidated Talking Machine Company (later the Victor Company) of Camden, New Jersey in 1900. The trademark depicted on these labels was adopted from Barraud's painting—for

*There is another version of the story recounting that the original painting featured Barraud's brother in the background stretched out in an open coffin. At Barraud's request, the Gramophone Company had lent him a shiny new instrument for the picture. After viewing the picture, the company was so pleased that they bought it on the condition that Barraud delete the gory background.

94

which the Consolidated Company, an associate company of the Gramophone· Company held the United States copyright.

Nipper soon became one of the world's best known trademarks. He promoted his product on signs, packaging and accessories. Later, the managing director of the Gramophone Company gave strict orders that in case of fire, the first thing the company's firemen were to do was to carry out the original painting from its place of honor on the wall of the director's board room.

Greyhound Bus Co.'s Greyhound

The world famous Greyhound Bus Company had its humble beginnings in the Mesabi Iron Ore Range in Minnesota. It was there, in 1914, that Carl E. Wickman opened an agency for the Hupmobile automobile. Unable to make a go of the business and rather than return to his job as a diamond drill operator, he used a seven passenger Hupmobile to transport miners between the small towns of Hibbing and Alice. The small bus line soon caught on and proved to be very popular with the miners. Wickman quickly purchased another Hupmobile, converted it into a nine passenger bus and the line's route was extended.

Because of dusty road conditions in those early days, the buses were painted battleship grey. The addition of extra seats to the touring cars had given them an extremely long, slim look. One day, an innkeeper whose hotel was located along the route remarked to Carl Wickman that the buses looked like "greyhound dogs streaking by." The name caught on, and Wickman adopted the slogan "Ride the Greyhounds." Today, Greyhound is the world's largest inter-city passenger carrier and chalks up over half a billion miles every year!

Although the Greyhound name is now almost synonymous with inter-city buses, the corporation has diversified into many new lines. Except for the strong image the name has achieved with one important sector of the company's total audience, the greyhound, by now, might have disappeared!

Fig. 35. *The Greyhound Bus Greyhound.*
    Courtesy, *The Greyhound Corporation*

Buster Brown's Tige

Buster Brown and his dog Tige, created in 1902, are still going strong as the Brown Shoe Company's trademark. Created by Richard F. Outcault, the Walt Disney of the early 1900's, Buster Brown, in his modish Lord Fauntleroy suit, was the incongruous source of endless mischief in which his sister Mary Jane and his dog Tige were lively co-conspirators.

Inspired by Outcault's children and their Boston bulldog, the comic strip caught the imagination of John A. Bush, a young sales executive in the Brown Shoe Company of St. Louis. To Bush, the little comic strip character seemed to have been born to be the living, selling trademark for his firm's line of children's shoes. Bush talked to Outcault and arranged for the Brown Shoe Company to use the Buster Brown logotype. At the St. Louis World's Fair of 1904, a new collection of Buster Brown shoes was prominently featured.

John Bush had overlooked one major point—he had not contracted for

Fig. 36. *Brown Shoe Company's Buster Brown Logo.*

Courtesy, *Brown Group, Inc.*

96

exclusive rights to Buster Brown. Cartoonist Outcault, now aware of the merchandising value of a comic strip character, had rented a booth of his own at the fair and soon Buster Brown and his dog would appear on scores of other products—from cigars to bourbon.

Bush was undaunted and hired a midget and dog to tour the country promoting Buster Brown shoes. Along the way, he wore out five dogs! Always the act would say: "I'm Buster Brown; I live in a shoe, (WOOF! WOOF!) that's my dog Tige; he lives there too." Just as Aunt Jemima became a "real" person, Buster Brown, with Bush's insight, became another "living" trademark. Today, the Brown Shoe Company is a member of the Brown Group, Inc., a diversified manufacturer and retailer of footwear, fabrics and speciality apparel. Buster Brown is still used as the trademark for the firm's line of children's shoes.

Camel

In the trademark zoo, the camel is quickly associated with the R.J. Reynolds' world-famous cigarettes—Camels. Created in 1913 by R.J. Reynolds, a Winston-Salem tobacco merchant, the cigarettes were named to project orientalism (a current vogue), its Turkish tobacco content and because the name was also easy to say and remember.

Around the turn of the century, machine-made cigarettes contained mostly Virginian or Turkish tobacco, neither of which proved very popular when offered to the roll-your-own buyer. Reynolds concluded that a blended cigarette was needed and decided to market test four separate brands. Reyno, Osman, Red Kamel (straight Turkish cut) and Camel were chosen. The new brand Camel decisively outsold the others, persuading Reynolds to move directly into national distribution.

Taking great pains with the Camel package design, Reynolds now urgently sought a rather appealing camel to grace his package. Luckily, by chance, the world famous Barnum & Bailey Circus was touring near Winston-Salem and, as the story goes, R.C. Haberkern, Reynolds' stenographer, persuaded them to allow their dromedary, "Old Joe," to be photographed for use on the pack design. The circus manager took a rather dim view of the young man with the camera and loudly complained that the entire incident was foolish. Haberkern gently reminded him that Reynolds had closed its factory and given its employees a holiday just so they could attend the circus. The manager quickly relented and offered his cooperation.

Old Joe would not keep still for his photograph, so his trainer hit him on the nose with a stick. Outraged, Old Joe pulled back his ears, raised his tail,

Fig. 37. *Old Joe.* The model for "Camel" cigarettes packaging, shown here in an old photograph.

Courtesy, *R.J. Reynolds Tobacco Co.*

and adopted a posture signifying offended dignity. It was this pose that was recorded for posterity.

A drawing was made from this photograph and the artist added the palms and pyramids in the background to project the Oriental idea. Camel brand cigarettes were ready for market in 1913 and in the following year alone Reynolds sold 425 million Camel cigarettes. By 1921, Camel cigarettes hit the 18 billion mark, accounting for about half the market total, and cigarettes, for the first time, became the best selling of all tobacco products.

The rather bold use of a Camel as a trademark for cigarettes was both innovative and unique. Scores of cigarette manufacturers, worldwide, imitated Camel's outstanding successes (see Table 6.3). In addition there were Derby (donkey—Paraguay), Monroe (stag—Brazil), Emu (emu—Costa Rica) and Giraffe (giraffe—Malaysia) brand cigarettes soon on the market. Also appearing were several additional brands that blatantly projected both the imagery of the pyramid and the picture of a Camel (Canada, Kamel and Camel Rider).

TABLE 6.3

OTHER ANIMAL BRAND CIGARETTES

Nation	Brand
India	Bat
China	Elephant, Golden Horse, Flying Horse, Dog's Head, Golden Sparrow, Xiongmao (Panda)
Canada	Mallard
U.K.	Tiger, Black Cat (Cat), Robin, Golden Butterfly, White Swans, Monkey
Japan	Glory (Rooster)
Malaya	Three Geese, Teddy Bear
U.S.S.R.	Mosselprom (Horses and cows)
Australia	Kookaburra (Kiwi bird)
U.S.A.	Camel

COW

In the 1930's the dairy industry had its share of public relations and consumer problems. Well-publicized "milk wars" that were raging between farmers and dairy processors caused the big dairies in particular to be pictured frequently as evil moneymakers off both the farmers and the public. Borden concluded the best approach was a friendly one, and one that would cause people to laugh or at least smile.

The most difficult of all proving grounds was selected as a test for this new kind of advertising: the then extremely dignified medical journals. In 1936 Borden's launched the medical advertising series that was to result in the creation of Elsie the Borden Cow. These were by no means "Elsie ads"; they were ads featuring a variety of cartoon cows with a variety of names, including Mrs. Blossom, Bessie, Clara . . . Elsie. A typical ad showed a cow and calf talking in a milking barn:

Calf: "Mama, I think I see a germ!"
Cow: "Mercy child—run quick for the Borden Inspector."

Another pictured a group of young heifers hanging on the words of a rather lazy and unimpressive-looking cow:

Heifers: "And now tell us about the time you got kicked out by Borden's."

99

Doctors loved the ads and swamped the company with requests for reprints to hand out in office waiting rooms. While the medical campaign continued, Borden also began testing it in a few New York area newspapers. But it was in 1938 that Elsie came to real life coast to coast in both the U.S. and Canada. Borden was then sponsoring a network news commentator named Rush Hughes. A radio copywriter, intrigued by one of the medical journal ads, prepared a commercial that so delighted Hughes he read it himself. It made reference to the following letter:

> Dear Mama:
> I'm so excited I can hardly chew. We girls are sending our milk to Borden's now!
> Love,
> Elsie

That commercial so amused Hughes' listeners that fan mail began coming in addressed not to him but to Elsie. Elsie became the spokescow for Borden ever after.

By 1939 Elsie had made her debut in national consumer magazines and had been quickly adopted by all the company's milk plants as a feature of local community promotional programs. She even made an appearance on a bottle cap. And on the air she and Rush Hughes continued their regular correspondence. Borden was then preparing to open a very fancy, scientifically important exhibit at the New York World's Fair, and it seemed only natural to include a few cartoons of Elsie at the exhibit. However, she was not to be the focal point. That was a new "rotolactor," a kind of merry-go-round where cows were automatically milked on a 360° cycle. It was all very agricultural and very futuristic. Seven young hostesses had been trained to answer every scientific question and were instructed to keep logs of the questions most often asked. At the first month's end the tally was:

- 20% about the rotolactor
- 20% about the location of the rest rooms
- 60% about which of the 150 cows was Elsie.

Elsie's popularity was confirmed, and it was obvious Borden was going to disappoint a lot of friends if it couldn't produce a real Elsie, and fast. Of all the cows in the exhibit, the most beautiful was a seven-year-old blueblooded Jersey from Brookfield, Massachusetts, whose registered name was "You'll Do, Lobelia"—a name which would come back to haunt Borden some twenty years later. For the rest of the season, this particular Elsie, dressed in a beautifully embroidered green blanket, was put all alone on the rotolactor twice each day for all to see, and millions did. This was a time when Borden advertising people learned something else: most cows are natural hams if

100

Fig. 38. *Elsie the Borden Cow.*
Courtesy, *Borden, Inc.*

given the opportunity, and Lobelia was among the hammiest. She didn't just smile at the crowds; she gave every impression of counting the house. The public took her to their hearts. That is how the live Elsie was born.

There is a misconception that Elsie went out of favor and was "brought back." Elsie never has been gone. She has appeared on many of Borden's product packages during the past few years and was featured along with the rest of her family during a 1976 Bicentennial advertising campaign. The live Elsie has been seen by thousands during the past few years at shopping malls and trade show sites. Although she may not be as visible today, when Borden is more a chemical company, than she was in the 40s, when the dairy side of the business was dominant, she most certainly was not shelved by Bordens.

Other members of the bovine family have also served as product trademarks. Over the years these have included Colman's Bull's Head, Bull Durham's famous bull and even more recently Nieman-Marcus' Red River brand (a Texas steer).

CAT

Ever since the time of the ancient Egyptians the image of a cat has graced many objects—from furniture to cigarettes. But perhaps the most famous cat of all appears on the Carreras' Black Cat cigarette package. The fantastic success of the cat for Carreras Ltd (U.K.) has been responsible for the cat's use for other packages and firms—Chick, Black Cat, Craven A and Black Cat No. 9 (son of Black Cat).

Although the black cat represents good luck, there was actually a black cat in Carreras' Wardour Street premises. Customers called the shop the "Black Cat Shop" so the name came to be closely associated with the firm and was included on early packaging. Even the entrance to Carreras' famous Arcadia plant was flanked by two giant statues of a black cat!

In addition to Black Cat brand cigarettes in the U.K., there is Schwarze Katz (Germany) brand cigarettes and Schwarze Katz (Germany) brand wines, as well as many other cat brand products.

Animals as trademarks do create a specially induced mood for a package. The grandeur of eagles has been an inspiration since the Paleolithic Era when drawings of the creatures first appeared in European caves. The birds came to symbolize courage, authority, power, freedom and immortality. Eagles served as emblems of the Babylonian empire, Charlemagne, the Caesars, many Holy Roman and Byzantine emperors, Napoleon and the czars of Russia. It was the bird of Jove, the god of gods. In *Packaging: The Sixth Sense* (Cahners Books, 1975), Dr. Ernest Dichter says "A look of determination created by the tightly closed muscles around the beak of an eagle have led to the erroneous symbolic interpretation that we are dealing with a very resolute and courageous animal. Apparently, millions of people of completely varying cultures interpreted this expression similarly and chose the eagle as their symbol for a whole country or for special products. There must be literally thousands of companies, such as Eagle clothes, Eagle tools, that use an eagle in their package design."

TABLE 6.4

ANIMALS AS SYMBOLS (U.S.)

Animal	Symbol
Lamb	Meekness
Lion	Courage
Owl	Wisdom
Eagle	Determination
Cat	Luck
Fox	Slyness
Dove	Peace
Bee	Activity
Donkey	Resolution
Penguin	Dirt
Turtle	Hardness, slowness
Rabbit	Quickness

102

7

THE WORLD OF MAKE BELIEVE: COINED NAMES

"The letter K had been a favorite with me—it seemed a strong, incisive sort of letter. Therefore it became a question of trying out a great number of combinations of letters that made words starting and ending with K. The word Kodak *is the result."*
George Eastman (1920)
in *System Magazine*

Fabricated or "made-up" names have been used as product trademarks for many years. In *Modern Advertising* (1909), Calkins and Holden state, "A coined word is a word made up expressly as a name for a particular article as a means of identifying it. It can be protected by copyright so that no other man can use it as applied to that particular article. Sapolio, Uneeda, Zu Zu are all examples of coined names." There are other, more recent examples of fabricated names for famous products such as Zonite, Marfak, Dreft and Yuban. The name Kodak, intended to represent a line of cameras made by the Eastman Kodak Company (Rochester, N.Y.), is certainly one of the most widely used coined names. It is also considered to be one of the best examples of an arbitrary and coined mark.

Kodak

"You press the button, we do the rest."
Eastman Kodak Slogan (1880's)

The innovations introduced by George Eastman and the Eastman Kodak Company, in all its various forms, mark some of the most important phases in the development of photographic science. Eastman's earliest steps in the field

of photography were in the production of the sensitive plates that early pho-
tographers used to record their images, and it would seem that it was his
desire to market these, and later roll films, that led to the development of all
the many Kodak cameras.

Eastman began the manufacture of photographic plates in about 1880,
but by 1885 he had succeeded in finding a way in which the light sensitive
emulsion used to record the image could be coated onto paper. This development meant that film, or Eastman Negative Paper as it was called, could be
sold in rolls, thereby enabling the photographer to take several exposures
without reloading his camera—as was necessary when using individual plates.
It was a later improvement in this film that allowed Eastman to introduce his
first camera, known simply as The Kodak.

The Kodak was a simple box camera, and it was first marketed in 1888.
The Kodak, for the first time, made photography available to anyone able to
afford the purchase price of $25. It came complete with a load of roll film
sufficient for 100 exposures—which, incidentally, yielded circular negatives.
When the user had made his 100 exposures the camera was returned to the
factory where the film was taken out, processed and printed. The camera was
returned to the owner with a new load of film to be followed, a couple of
weeks later, by the prints from his first load.

It was this simple processing system, as much as any other factor, that
made Eastman's introduction a true revolution in the field of photography.
Before this time any photographer also had to be something of a chemist. In
fact, this development led to what is now known as 'snapshotting'—taking
photographs of family events etc., simply to record their happening, rather
than attempting to create works of art.

Needing a name for his new product, Eastman simply made up one,
"Kodak." He coined the name as being one which could be easily pronounced in any language, and one unlike any other trade name—but it has
no meaning, nor does it derive from any root words.

Eastman later said, "I chose that name because I knew a trade name
must be short, vigorous, incapable of being misspelled to an extent that will
destroy its identity, and, in order to satisfy trademark laws, it must mean
nothing." It is ironic that Eastman studied the dictionary in vain to find a
name for his new camera, since the word he eventually coined is now in all
dictionaries.

George Eastman's trade name was so successful that it was soon in dan-
ger of becoming a generic name. To combat this trend, the company adopted
the slogans, "Only Eastman makes the Kodak" and "If it isn't an Eastman, it
isn't a Kodak." To further enhance its corporate history, the curled print

Fig. 39. *George Eastman.*
Courtesy, *Eastman Kodak
Company*

trademark was added.

The first Kodak was an enormous commercial success, although examples of this model are now comparatively rare. Close on the heels of the original camera came the Kodak No. 2, which took slightly larger photographs, and in 1890 this was followed by the Nos. 3 and 4, and the Nos. 3 and 4 Junior. All of these were loaded with films by the factory, as they had to be loaded in the dark—a skill which Eastman felt was beyond the capabilities, or inclinations, of most users. The next three box cameras the company introduced were known as Ordinary Kodaks and with these, for the first time, Eastman allowed users to load their own cameras—albeit in the darkroom.

Then, in 1895, a further model was added to the range. This was the Pocket Kodak—a box camera of minute size which used film based on celluloid but with a paper backing that allowed it to be loaded in daylight. Eastman called this Cartridge Film, although its modern counterpart is known as roll.

Once this new film had been introduced, a great rash of models followed, each allowing the user to load his own camera in daylight. Best known among these were the Brownie range introduced in 1900, and the Bullet and Bull's Eye dating from the mid-1890's. Alongside these simple box cameras

Eastman introduced a slightly more advanced range known as Folding Kodaks in 1890. These early box cameras established a tradition, and for the next 40 years or so few families were complete without their Kodak. This has meant that there are now literally dozens of different models for the collector to seek—and almost all of these are still inexpensive.

Although his introduction of simple photography had effectively taken the western world by storm, Eastman was not content to rest on his laurels. Having encouraged the average man-in-the-street to take up photography, he next led him on to a deeper involvement with the introduction of a slightly more complex design. Just as the box Kodaks were copied by almost every camera maker in the world, so the Folding Pocket Kodak was to establish a trend in camera manufacture that was to last until well after the Second World War.

The Eastman Kodak Company is still a world leader in the field of photography and a prime mover in the use of sophisticated advertising. After all, if a coined word such as Kodak is used as the selling power behind a product, intelligent advertising must be used to project the name in front of the public.

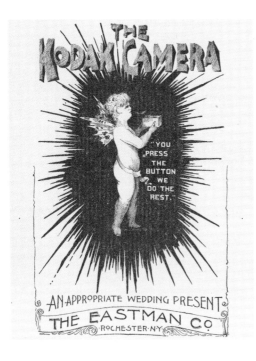

Fig. 40. *An Appropriate Wedding Present.* An early advertisement featuring a George Eastman slogan.
Courtesy, *Eastman Kodak Company*

106

Yuban

The name Yuban was selected by John Arbuckle, a well-known coffee merchant and connoisseur of fine coffee. At Christmas time, it was Arbuckle's custom to serve his own special blend of coffee to guests. The blend was not available anywhere else except at Arbuckle's house.

Arbuckle referred to his annual holiday dinner as this "Yuletide Banquet," and the coffee he served was known as Yu Ban. For many years, this story was believed to be how Yuban brand coffee was named. But there is a truer version of the origin of the name Yuban.

On green coffee shipments to Arbuckle Brothers, New York, the bags containing the beans were marked ABNY (for Arbuckle Brothers, New York). When a brand name was to be chosen, an effort was made to form a word out of the letters on the bags. Combinations like Bany and Naby were discarded as not euphonious. Yban looked somewhat strange, until someone suggested adding the letter u to it—and the name Yuban was born!

Other Names

There are literally hundreds of other coined names in everyday use. Häagen-Dazs brand ice cream means nothing in Danish or in any other language, but to millions of ice cream connoisseurs it translates to the creamiest, richest and best tasting summer treat in the land. So why the umlaut and the map of Scandinavia on the lid? "We wanted people to take a second look and say, 'Is this imported?' " admits the firm's founder and president, Reuben Mattus. His wife, Rose, thought it up. "We made a name and created a meaning for it. It means 'the best.' "

Another example is the name Exxon. Two of the best known brands of gasoline and oil are Esso (introduced in 1926) and Enco (introduced in 1960), which represent the products of Standard Oil of New Jersey and its Humble Oil subsidiary. The result of an effort to find a new single brand name was Exxon, whose basic appeal is explained by *Time* (October 25, 1971) as, "It says nothing and it means nothing" (see Table 7.1).*

Ever since the 1911 breakup of the Standard Oil trust, legal restrictions have barred any firm from using the name Standard nationally—or even the name Esso (which comes from S.O.). Jersey Standard had to operate Esso stations in the East, while Humble stations were in Ohio and Enco stations else-

---

*It has also been suggested that Exxon was chosen because of the similarity with former President Nixon just as Mr. Clean was the kind of man one associated with President Eisenhower (Dichter, *Packaging: The Sixth Sense*, Cahners Books, 1976).

Fig. 41. *New Exxon Sign.*

Courtesy, *Exxon*

TABLE 7.1

VARIOUS CORPORATE NAME CHANGES

Original Name	New Name
South Penn Oil Co.	Pennzoil Co.
Tennessee Gas Transmission Co.	Tenneco, Inc.
Pittsburgh Plate Glass Co.	PPG
Radio Corporation of America	RCA Corp.
American Brake Shoe and Foundry Co.	Abex Corp.
Rexall Drug & Chemical Co.	Dart Industries Corp.
Haloid – Xerox	Xerox Corp.
R. J. Reynolds Tobacco Co.	R. J. Reynolds Industries Inc.
Libby–Owens–Ford Glass Co.	Libby–Owens–Ford Co.
Cudahy Packing Co.	Cudahy Co.
Socony Mobil Oil Co.	Mobil Oil Corp.
Allied Chemical Corp.	Allied Corp.
United Aircraft	United Technologies
Chemical Bank New York Trust Co.	Chemical Bank
Cleve Trust of Cleveland	Ameri-Trust
National Bank of Commerce of Seattle	Ranier Bank
First International Bancshares	InterFirst
Alabama Bancorporation	AmSouth

108

where. But this was no way to build strong national brand consciousness. In their search for a new name, Esso executives worked in absolute secrecy. To ensure security, they typed their own letters and memos. The project even had a code name, Operation Nugget.

The search team considered thousands of possibilities, including meaningless letter combinations clacked out by computers. Because the new trademark might eventually become global, one of the company's existing names, Enco, was quickly discarded. In Japanese, it means "stalled car." At last, after polling 7,000 customers and testing names in 55 languages, the company chose the computer-selected name, Exxon. It is short, quickly recognized, easily remembered and easy to pronounce. The double "x," except for proper names such as Foxx and Oxx, occurs only in the Maltese language. The estimated cost of research, advertising and physically changing the name on signs and other items was about $100 million.

Fig. 42. *Changeover Complete.* A 1973 photo of a service station that had just completed the name change.

Courtesy, *Exxon*

8
THE OLD FAMILY NAMES

"There are the Rockwell Rockwells, the Hallmark Halls, the Heinz Heinzes, and the Stevenses of J. P. Stevens. There are the Watsons of I.B.M. the Luces of Time and the Hunts, Murchisons, and Klebergs of Texas. But America's greatest industrial dynasties still come down to four names: du Pont, Mellon, Rockefeller and Ford."
New York Times (Oct. 25, 1981)

Many of the old familiar product brand names are derived from family names—Kraft cheeses, Heinz pickles, Ford cars, Campbell soups and Smith Brothers cough drops. But there are thousands of other families that have lent their names to scores and scores of different products. Their stories often reflect "a little bit of Americana" to the reader. Just consider the story of Oscar Mayer. The company was named after one of three brothers from Bavaria who started making weiner sausages in their neighborhood meat market in the 1880's. In 1929, the weiners were given the name Oscar Mayer. It's now one of America's favorite foods, inspired by its now-famous jingle:

Oh, I wish I were an Oscar Mayer Weiner.
That is what I'd truly like to be,
'cause if I were an Oscar Mayer Weiner,
everyone would be in love with me.

Henry J. Heinz Co.

It set me thinking. I said to myself, 'we do not have styles of products, but we do have varieties of products.' Counting up how many we had, I counted well beyond 57, but '57' kept coming back into my mind. 'Seven, seven'—there are so many illustra-

tions of the psychological influence of that figure
and of its alluring significance to people of all ages.
Fifty-eight Varieties, or 59 Varieties did not appeal to
me—just '57 Varieties'. When I got off the train, I
immediately went down to the lithographer's where
I designed a street-car ad and had it distributed
throughout the United States. I did not realize then,
of course, how successful it was going to be.

Henry J. Heinz

Henry J. Heinz was born of Bavarian immigrants in Sharpsburg, Pennsylvania in 1844. Although his family wanted young Henry to study for the ministry, he somehow became more interested in his mother's vegetable garden and, together, they cultivated their back yard. By the time he was 12 years old, Henry was already selling the surplus produce at a tidy little profit. At 16, he was making three deliveries a week and had developed a chain of customers. Late in the evening he would load his wagon, then go to bed until three in the morning when he would start for Pittsburgh, an hour's journey away.

After several other ventures, Henry decided that his future lay in the food business. In 1869, he formed a partnership with L. C. Noble. One of their first prepared products was bottled horseradish. At that time, housewives who wanted horseradish had to buy the roots and then shred them to make the sauce. It was a laborious task as the root was as hard on the eyes as were onions. The small amount of commercially available horseradish was being packed in green bottles to disguise the dishonest practice of using turnip fillers. The partnership of Heinz and Noble began with the cultivation of three-quarters of an acre of horseradish, which they packed in clear bottles.

After two years, Heinz added celery sauce and pickles to his line and fairly soon, his original three-quarters of an acre of horseradish had expanded to over 100 acres of farmland.

The panic of 1873 caused problems for the young company. Although the firm weathered the panic, it became bankrupt several years later. A short time after this bankruptcy, Henry once again formed a small company to process foods. With total capital of $3,000, the business was launched on February 6, 1876 under the name F. and J. Heinz, the initials for the brother and cousin who had contributed capital.

One of the first products introduced was ketchup. Making the sauce at home was a tedious task for the housewife. It involved heating the sauce in an iron kettle all day with constant stirring so the pulp would not adhere to the bottom of the kettle. Clearly a prepared ketchup would fill a gap in the market!

Fig. 43. *Keystone Ketchup Bottle.* Bottle #63 was hand blown and held 12 oz. (1890–1900). Courtesy, *H.J. Heinz Co.*

The Romans had a sauce called garum which closely resembled ketchup. But the word ketchup came from the Chinese ke-tsiap, a brine of pickled fish or shell fish, and the Malayan fish sauce kichop. Discovered by English sailors in the seventeenth century, it was brought home to England where it was recreated and extensively used.

Henry Heinz always insisted on the spelling that is closer to the original, ketchup, although others commonly call it catsup.

The widely known Heinz trademark, 57 Varieties, originated in 1896 when Henry was riding in an elevated train in New York City. Among the advertising cards in the train was one extolling the virtues of a brand of shoes that offered "21 styles." Although his firm was producing more than "57 Varieties" (there were more than 60 varieties at the time), he decided, rather unaccountably, that 57 was a lucky figure. In 1900, New York City's first elec-

*The H.J. Heinz Company discontinued the use of Heinz 57 in 1969, because it was making some 1,250 different "Varieties", had acquired companies with other brand names, and needed a broader corporate identity.

Fig. 44. *Henry J. Heinz ca. 1910.*
Courtesy, *H. J. Heinz Co.*

tric sign, advertised the "57 Varieties" with the outline of the Heinz pickle at the top. A new trademark had been born!* Today, the H.J. Heinz Company is one of the leading food processors in the world. This industrial giant now owns more than twenty worldwide companies and employs over 40,000 people. Robert C. Albers states in *The Good Provider* (Houghton Mifflin Co., 1973), "The history of the past century has not been so kind to Henry Heinz's social philosophy. It is now considered naive and simplistic to believe that the possibilities for improving the moral and intellectual condition of mankind by education are unlimited, or that virtue and happiness are sure to follow an advance in material well-being, or that (in Heinz's words) "there is an increasing brotherhood and a nobler manhood among the peoples of the earth," or that teaching the Golden Rule may bring universal peace among nations. But given the opportunity, Henry Heinz might observe gently that the road of upward progress has always been painful and beset with reversals, that the world is young, and that the last word is not yet in on man's struggle against ignorance, stupidity and evil."

Procter and Gamble

*"All thy garments smell of myrrh, and aloes, and
cassia, out of the ivory palaces, whereby they have
made thee glad."*

Psalms 45:8

In Cincinnati, in the year 1837, two men went into business as partners
at the suggestion of their father-in-law. William Procter was a candlemaker
and James Gamble, a soap boiler. The firm prospered and by 1859 the factory
had 80 employees and annual sales totaled $1 million.

In 1878 Procter and Gamble (P&G) perfected a formula for a revolutionary new hard soap. It was white and pure and it floated. Based on experiments with a formula for a soap without expensive olive oil, the new mixture
was poured into a blending machine. Apparently a workman forgot to shut
off the power when he went to lunch. When he returned, he shipped out the
batch in the hope that his negligence would go unnoticed. Customers who
received the accidental batch called for "more of that floating soap." The
company surmised that the intensive whipping had beat air into the mixture
and as a result the "soap floated."

Fig. 45. *Harley Procter.* Harley Procter, son of the
co-founder of Procter &
Gamble, was the genius behind the original marketing
of Ivory Soap. He designed
the wrapper and the
"notch," found the name
during a Psalms reading and
the statistics of the famous
purity slogan buried in dry
scientific evaluations, and
convinced the company
to spend a then unprece-
dented $11,000 for national
advertising.

Courtesy, *Procter and
Gamble Co.*

Somewhat on the conservative side, P&G called its new product, "The White Soap." This was considered too simple a name by Harley Procter and he decided to search for a new name that was truly reflective of the product. It came to him one Sunday morning in church.

Different men think of different matters when they sit in church. James Boswell indulged in reveries about beautiful women. Harley Procter thought about soap. As Procter was sitting in church listening to the minister's sermon, his mind wandered constantly to the problem of his still nameless soap. Suddenly he became aware of the words the minister was reading from Psalms 45:8. "Out of the ivory palaces . . . . . whereby they have made thee glad. . . ."

The new White Soap was successfully christened Ivory. It was trade-marked on July 18, 1879, and Procter now sought scientific evidence backing its claim of purity. After sending samples for analysis out to various college laboratories, he triumphantly boasted for his soap "It Floats" and claimed it was 99-44/100ths pure (a refreshing change from everybody else's "absolutely pure").

By advertising Ivory extensively, P&G became committed to brand-name marketing, large-scale advertising and the mass production of consumer goods.

Fig. 46. *Ivory Centennial.* The straightforward message, "Ivory Soap. It Floats," appeared chiseled in granite in this 1900 advertisement.
Courtesy, *Procter and Gamble Co.*

115

Hallmark Cards, Inc.

"I'd like to be the kind of a friend you've been to me."

Edgar A. Guest (from the first
sentimental card produced by
Hall Bros.)

The American greeting-cards business was started by Joyce C. Hall, a Kansas City, Mo. stationery dealer. At eighteen, young Joyce Hall became a wholesaler of postcards, Christmas cards and valentines. After a fire destroyed his initial plant, Joyce, with the help of his brother Rollie, not only rebuilt the business but acquired an engraving plant and, by 1915, began to market the first two Hall Brothers greeting cards. These first cards were manufactured unfolded with handpainted decorative symbols.

In 1916, the first sentimental message card was published by Hall and with that card the entire "social expression" type cards were launched.

By 1923 the name Hallmark became the only signature on the card and in 1954, it became the official name of the company. In the 1940's, Ed Goodman, Joyce Hall's sales and advertising manager coined the now-famous slogan, "When you care enough to send the very best." Mr. Hall liked the sound of the slogan and it made its debut in 1944, to fantastic acclaim.

The success of Hallmark in the marketplace was basically due to the quality image the Hall Brothers maintained and their personal feeling that "good taste is good business."

Reynolds Metals Co.

"That highly valued metal has . . . . the tenacity of iron, the fusibility of copper, the light weight of glass; it is easily worked, it is extremely wide-spread in nature . . . . it is three times lighter than iron. . ."

Jules Verne

Reynolds Metals Company today is the second largest producer of primary aluminum in the United States, and the third largest in the world. The story of its phenomenal growth is inspiring as well as interesting; inspiring, because it shows what the faith and courage of one man can do; interesting, because it represents the development of an industry that is itself a comparative youngster.

The early history of Reynolds Metals, as well as that of its parent, U.S.

116

Foil Company, is really the history of one man. Richard Samuel Reynolds, Sr., was born in Bristol, Tennessee in 1881. His early experience with his uncle's tobacco business aroused his interest in the production of metal foil, and in 1919 he founded the U.S. Foil Company, whose first plant was in Louisville, Kentucky. Primary products of this company were tin and lead foil for packaging cigarettes and other tobacco items.

Within the next seven years, this young company developed several products and processes that were to be of tremendous importance in its later growth. The year 1921 saw the first letterpress printing on foil, an operation previously considered impractical. During the same year, the first foil-laminated cartons were made, and in the next two years, U.S. Foil introduced advanced methods of foil production that greatly lowered production costs. Eskimo Pie Corporation, which became a Foil affiliate in 1924, was one of the first to establish the protective quality of foil in the packaging of food products.

Aluminum was first introduced to U.S. Foil in 1926. This new metal, then selling for about 18¢ per pound after its World War I peak of 60¢, showed great potential as a packaging material for several reasons. First, it could be rolled to thinner foil and hence was less expensive because of greater yield per pound of metal. Then it was more brilliant, therefore more attractive. And it soon proved that its protective qualities were greater than either tin or lead, and it was much lighter. So in this year of 1926, Mr. Reynolds produced his first aluminum foil, the forerunner of the familiar Reynolds Wrap.

Under the far-seeing eye of R. S. Reynolds, Sr., Reynolds Metals Company was formed in 1928, primarily to provide a more flexible corporate structure for the rapidly growing business. Also in that year, the Company began the manufacture of aluminum powders.

During the next decade, Reynolds Metals Company expanded and prospered. Many technical developments increased both the quality and the quantity of Reynolds products, such as high-speed rotogravure color printing on foil. In 1937, the Company received an order for 100 million beer labels, the largest such order ever placed up to that time. By 1940, sales were at an annual rate of $20 million.

But all the metal Reynolds was using had to be bought, and there was only one primary producer in the United States. In 1938, Mr. Reynolds made a trip to Europe to find other suppliers for aluminum. He was able to purchase primary ingot in France, but he was concerned that despite Germany's tremendous increase in aluminum metal production, she had none available for sale. To him the motive was obvious. Germany was preparing for a light metals war, and this meant an air war.

117

Returning to the United States, Mr. Reynolds tried for months to persuade both industry and government to increase domestic primary aluminum production. But everywhere he turned the answer was the same: we have plenty of aluminum for any possible demand.

But Reynolds Metals Company was not satisfied. Not only was more aluminum vital to meet the military needs of the United States, but the Company also needed its own source of metal to eliminate its dependence on other suppliers.

And so a historic decision was made: Reynolds Metals Company would become a primary aluminum producer. This was in April, 1940. The next few months were spent raising money and selecting building sites. The firm knew that needed plants would cost millions of dollars. To raise this sum, Reynolds mortgaged not only all its existing plants but also all those to be built with the borrowed funds.

On November 20, 1940, ground was broken near Sheffield, Alabama, for a reduction plant. Just two days less than six months later, on May 18, 1941, Reynolds poured its first aluminum ingot—a construction record that still stands. In the meantime, an alumina plant and sheet and rod mills were under construction at the same site, and another reduction plant was being built at Longview, Washington. At Louisville, Reynolds acquired a rod mill, a sheet mill and an extrusion plant. In Arkansas, Reynolds started to mine bauxite.

Thus, by 1942, when the U.S. was in desperate need of aluminum, Reynolds Metals had the capacity to produce it at a rate of about 100,000 tons a year. During the next three years, the Company furnished almost 500,000 tons of metal in the form of prefabricated airplane parts, radio and radar equipment, and other vital military supplies.

After the war, many people felt that this tremendous capacity to produce aluminum could not be absorbed by civilian demand for at least five years. Not only had Reynolds capacity been greatly enlarged, but a number of government-owned plants had been built and operated during the war years, and other primary facilities had been increased.

But again Reynolds disagreed with the "experts" as it had a few years earlier. In this case, it believed that civilian demand could be so stimulated that the excess capacity could be used without delay. A proposal was submitted to lease, with options to buy, six government-owned plants; this proposal was accepted.

Under this agreement, these plants were leased to Reynolds in 1946, and in 1949 the Company purchased them. They were: in Hurricane Creek, Arkansas, an alumina plant; in Jones Mills, Arkansas, and in Troutdale, Oregon, reduction plants; a sheet rolling mill in McCook, Illinois; and extrusion

Fig. 47. *Consumers Meet "Reynolds Wrap."* The introduction of "Reynolds Wrap" in 1948 was a major household event. Note the reference to "pure aluminum" on the carton.

Courtesy, *Reynolds Metals Company*

plants in Grand Rapids, Michigan and Phoenix, Arizona.

The only justification for this peacetime expansion was the belief that adequate markets existed to absorb the increased production, and that the proper sales techniques could expand such markets. In 1947, the Company decided to spearhead the advertising and promotion of all its products with a new household foil, Reynolds Wrap. Although it wasn't until 1950 that household foil attained national distribution, 1947 marked the first introduction for many people to the versatile metal aluminum. The first and still most important consumer product, Reynolds Wrap, proved to be the key that opened the minds of millions of people as it did the doors of millions of homes to Reynolds Aluminum.

The Korean conflict in 1950 found Reynolds Metals Company with an annual primary production capacity of 230,000 tons. Again believing that this was not enough to meet the emergency demands for aluminum, the Company built new reduction plants near Corpus Christi, Texas and Arkadelphia, Arkansas, and added potlines at several existing plants. These new facilities nearly doubled U.S. primary capacity.

In 1948, R. S. Reynolds, Sr. had become Chairman of the Board of Reynolds Metals Company, and R. S. Reynolds, Jr. had been elected President. Mr. Reynolds, Sr. was to remain in this position, inspiring the firm in its vigorous growth, until his death in 1955.

The decade of the 50's was filled with significant technical advances. The first molten aluminum deliveries, whereby melted metal was delivered directly to customers' holding furnaces, were successfully completed in 1950. By 1952, bauxite was being shipped from both Jamaica and British Guiana (now Guyana). Do-It-Yourself Aluminum was added to the company's product line in 1953. Reynolds Tubed Sheet was introduced to the refrigeration industry in 1954, and in 1955 both aluminum strip conductor and Colorweld were placed on the market.

Reynolds entered the 60's with an annual primary capacity of over 700,000 tons. By 1964, this had been raised to 725,000 tons, and this expansion continued. In 1964, a $140-million plant additions and improvements program was started which increased primary capacity to 815,000 tons by 1967. Early in 1966, another plan was announced, under which $325 million would be spent in further increasing production and other facilities to bring primary capacity to 975,000 tons by 1970. Thus in six years, the Company invested over half a billion dollars in new plants and equipment, one proof of its faith in its future.

This growth in capacity, of course, had to be justified by an equivalent growth in markets. A continuing flow of new products, was the symbol of the 60's at Reynolds. Among growing markets, two of the most important were transportation and building products; together they accounted for some 45% of sales.

ST. GEORGE AND THE DRAGON (The story of the Reynolds Metals Co. trademark)

Little, if anything, is known of the life history of St. George. The legends concerning him have, however, grown throughout the centuries, and have developed into a romantic tapestry in which fact and fantasy are interwoven.

Legend asserts that he was born of noble Christian parents, probably about the middle of the third century, in Cappadocia in eastern Asia Minor. This was a Roman province, then under the rule of the emperor Diocletian. As a tribune or magistrate, St. George had the responsibility of protecting the individual plebian citizen from the arbitrary rulings of the patricians; essen-

120

tially, he was a defender of the people.

It is easy to see how legend could magnify this position from legal protector to a slayer of dragons. When George was martyred by Diocletian for his adherence to the Christian faith, the foundation was complete for his establishment as the great champion of good over evil. He was recognized as a saint by Pope Gelasius in 495.

In the middle of the 14th century, Edward III of England instituted an order of knighthood in honor of St. George, England's patron saint. This later became the Order of the Garter, perhaps the most famous of the British orders.

The legend of St. George's battle against the dragon first appears in the late 12th century. It was popularized by the 13th century "Golden Legend," a collection of exaggerated romantic accounts of the early Christians. The "Legend" served as inspiration for many of the medieval artists, including the Italian painter Raphael (1483-1520).

Raphael has been ranked with Michaelangelo and Leonardo as the greatest of the Italian painters. His "St. George and the Dragon," painted in 1504, was a favorite of R. S. Reynolds, Sr. The crusading spirit of St. George, as depicted in this painting, was an inspiration to Mr. Reynolds; the painting itself suggested the now-familiar KNIGHT-AND-DRAGON symbol of Reynolds Metals Company.

The original of this painting is in oil on wood paneling, and is signed by

Fig. 48. *Reynolds' "St. George and the Dragon" Trademark.*
Courtesy, *Reynolds Metals Company*

Fig. 49. *Reynolds' Inspiration.* A detail of the original painting by Raphael which served as the inspiration for the Reynolds trademark pictured above.
Courtesy, *Reynolds Metals Company*

the artist on the breastband of the horse's harness. It is a small painting, measuring only 11¼ by 8½ inches. During its 450-year history, it has belonged to a number of European royal collections, including the Russian from which Andrew Mellon purchased it. It now hangs as part of the Mellon Collection in Washington's National Gallery of Art.

McDonald's Corp.

"When you're green you're growing and when you're ripe you start to rot."
McDonald's founder Ray Kroc

In 1954, Ray Kroc visited a small drive-in restaurant in San Bernardino, Ca. operated by the McDonald Brothers. It was an offshoot of an earlier unit that both Maurice and Richard McDonald had closed in 1948. Kroc owned the rights to distribute Prince Castle Multi-Mix milk shake mixers world-wide and, intrigued by an order for eight mixers from a single restaurant, flew out to inspect the McDonald's drive-in.

Recognizing that the McDonald brothers had "something good" he persuaded them to allow him to franchise similar restaurants nationwide in exchange for 0.5 percent of the sales of the franchised restaurants. Kroc was to charge a royalty to the franchisees not to exceed 1.9 percent of their sales plus an initial franchise fee of $950. His profit potential was limited to 1.4 percent of sales. The first McDonald's restaurant was established in Des Plaines, Ill. on April 15, 1955. Art Bender was the McDonald's employee who sold the first hamburger.

In 1959, Harry Sonneborn became president of McDonalds and launched the corporation into the real estate business. Forming a separate corporation, Franchise Realty Corporation, for the purpose of finding and leasing sites to franchisees, the corporation later changed its name to McDonald's Corp. and one day later acquired all the outstanding stock of McDonald's System, Inc., which was the company that actually had the franchising agreement with the McDonald brothers.

In the 1960's, Kroc concentrated on developing franchised units. At the end of 1960, 225 units in the system were franchised. Ronald McDonald made his debut as a national symbol in 1966 replacing "Speedee," the original advertising trademark.

During the 1970's, the first store achieved sales volume of over $1 million. Initial overseas entries occurred—first in the Netherlands, then in Japan. In 1974, the chain's 3,000th store was opened in London, with the site representing the chain's initial entry into that country. Adding a roughly constant number of units (about 500) to a growing base of stores will necessarily reduce the growth rate in percentage terms in the future. However, systemwide sales and profit growth approaching 20 percent annually into the 1980's appears attainable.

Initially, McDonald's menu items centered around the hamburger and cheeseburger; however, with the widespread public acceptance of the fast-service concept, the company sought to appeal to a rapidly growing, diverse market by adding additional items to its original menu. Among these items are: the Filet-O-Fish sandwich, McDonald's first menu addition in 1965; The Big Mac sandwich, McDonald's most popular sandwich, 1968; the Quarter Pounder sandwich, 1972; McDonaldland Cookies, 1973; McDonald's sundaes, 1978. Since 1976, McDonald's has also served a complete line of breakfast items, featuring the Egg McMuffin sandwich, which was developed in 1973. McDonald's restaurant personnel receive special instruction in the latest food service techniques at Hamburger University, the firm's professional restaurant management training school. In the regions, restaurant crewmembers benefit from modern training facilities and methods, ranging from in-restaurant, on-the-job training to sophisticated audio visual training tools.

In spite of McDonald's not being the first fast food hamburger chain (see table 8.1), its success has been amazing. Since its initial stock offering in April, 1965, McDonald's stock has risen more than thirty times, which has created a personal net worth for founder Ray Kroc well in excess of a quarter of a billion dollars!

TABLE 8.1

FAST FOOD HAMBURGER CHAINS

Date Opened	Name
1921	White Castle
1923	White Tower
1925	Howard Johnson's
1935	Friendly Ice Cream Corp.
1941	Foodmaker (Jack-in-the-box)
1954	Burger King
1955	McDonald's
1969	Wendy's

Johnson and Johnson

*"I was determined to devise some manner of ban-
dage that would stay in place, be easily applied and
still retain its sterility."*

Earle E. Dickson
(Developer of Band-Aid)

Founded in 1885 by James Wood and Edward Mead Johnson, Johnson and Johnson (J&J) became operational the following year, when it produced nearly a dozen products, mostly medical plasters.

The first roll of surgical tape was sold in 1886 and then, in 1894, came the first consumer product—Johnson's Baby Powder. It was first sold in a tubular container. For years, baby powders were antiseptic. In 1910, an antiseptic perfumed talcum was marketed. Eventually, the federal government ruled that boric acid, the base of the antiseptic process, could no longer be used in baby products because it acted as an irritant. J&J is very selective in its source of talc for the powder and now owns a talc mine in Vermont.

The first cotton rolls were sold in 1887 and sterilized absorbent cotton was introduced five years later. These early products were not sold directly to the public. Rather they were sold to druggists, who then recommended products to their customers. Only in about 1916 did J&J begin any consumer advertising.

The first medicated plasters—ancestors of today's back plasters—were sold in cigar boxes that J&J purchased from a nearby New Brunswick factory. All J&J did was put its labels on the boxes.

The early plasters had trade names such as Hemlock and Bellcopsic that indicated the make-up of the plasters. Later, the company decided to change the brand names to reflect the various purposes for the plasters, such as for coughing and chest weaknesses.

The first tape was marketed as "an excellent adhesive with a rubber base," but unfortunately it tended to irritate sensitive skin. Late in the 19th century, zinc oxide was added to the adhesive to ease the irritation. A tape for hypo-allergenic people with sensitive skin later was developed. Called Dermicel, the tape has a permeable cloth backing that allows air to pass through.

BAND-AID ORIGIN

In 1920, Earle E. Dickson and his wife Josephine were newlyweds. Inexperienced in the kitchen, Mrs. Dickson frequently cut or burned her fingers while preparing meals at their home in New Brunswick, N.J. This unfortu-

124

nate propensity for minor accidents, while painful and distressing to the young bride, led to the invention of the BAND-AID Brand Adhesive Bandage—a product known today to consumers around the world.

Dickson, 28, a son and grandson of New England doctors, tenderly bandaged his wife's fingers with gauze and adhesive. These were products of the local Johnson & Johnson plant, where Dickson was employed as a cotton buyer in the purchasing department.

Despairing of ever achieving an accident-free kitchen, and tired of applying clumsy, easily lost bandages, Dickson sat down one night to give the matter some thought. He recalled: "I was determined to devise some manner of bandage that would stay in place, be easily applied, and still retain its sterility."

He conceived a new idea and decided to make up some bandages in advance of the next mishap. Strips of surgical tape, manufactured by Johnson & Johnson, were laid sticky-side up on a table. Then Dickson rolled up a pad of gauze bandage and stuck it on the middle of the tape and covered the tape and gauze with crinoline.

For every cut or burn, his bride would simply cut off a slice from the handy roll, peel off the crinoline, and apply the bandage. The added advantage was that she could do this herself without a neighbor's, or her hus-

Fig. 50. *Band-Aid Packages.*
A view of various Band-Aid packages through the years.
Courtesy, *Johnson and Johnson*

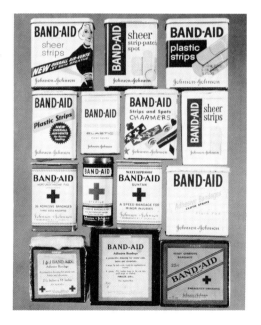

125

band's, helping hand.

Dickson mentioned his invention to a fellow employee at Johnson & Johnson, who encouraged him to tell his story to management. The idea was well received. The company's president, James W. Johnson, saw the potential for the new and unique bandage as a basic first aid product to protect wounds.

A decision was made to manufacture the product under the trademark of "BAND-AID," a name suggested by W. Johnson Kenyon, superintendent of the mill at the Johnson & Johnson plant.

The first adhesive bandages were made by hand and produced in sections three inches wide and 18 inches long. Removable crinoline protected the adhesive surface. The user scissored off as long a strip as was required.

At first sales were low, but believers in the new bandage persisted. One of these was Dr. Frederick B. Kilmer, father of Joyce Kilmer, the poet. In addition to heading the company's research department, Dr. Kilmer edited a Johnson & Johnson magazine for druggists. He became a leading advocate of the BAND-AID Brand Adhesive Bandage. In nearly every issue of the magazine he promoted the product as a means of preventing infection and speeding the healing of small injuries. Samples were given to Boy Scouts. A salesman distributed bandages to every butcher in Cleveland.

By 1924, further development of the bandage to meet consumer needs led to the design of machinery to precut three-inch by three-quarter-inch bandages. Business increased 50 percent that year.

The BAND-AID Brand Adhesive Bandage was a natural for the nation's and the world's medicine chests, hospitals, doctor's offices and first-aid kits. Physicians adopted them for protecting smallpox vaccinations. Among their many uses, they were found ideal for covering scratches and burns suffered by circus workers handling ropes and stakes.

Product improvements to BAND-AID Brand Adhesive Bandages have continued through the years. In 1928, aeration holes were added to the pad and later to the entire bandage to promote faster healing. Medicated bandages were introduced in 1928. The entire product was made sterile in 1939. BAND-AID Brand Plastic Strips were introduced in 1951, and Sheer Strips in 1958. The pad has also been improved to provide greater cushioning, absorption and fluid dispersion. Improvements will continue to be made to all parts of the BAND-AID Brand Adhesive Bandage as new bandaging technology is developed.

Earle E. Dickson, the inventor of this product, retired from the company in 1957. He was elected to the Johnson & Johnson Board of Directors in 1929, and was named a vice president in 1932. He died in 1962.

Gauze, one of the second wave of J & J products (about 1886–87), was rolled as a surgical dressing. The first gauze was antiseptically cleaned with carbolic acid vapors. About 1892, a dry heat or steam sterilization process was inaugurated. Moist gauze strips used to pack cavities were introduced the same year. Today, these are marketed as Nu Gauze.

The first sponges that J&J marketed were natural sponges that were carefully sterilized. Six years later, about 1905, the company began to make textile sponges.

Dental floss was introduced in 1899 and was packed in the same containers in which adhesive tape was sold. A half-century later, J&J began to make separate plastic containers.

First aid kits were first sold about 1888. One type was the Household Accident Case, but J&J also provided a larger wooden railway station and factory supply case, complete with a book of "what to do" instructions.

As the years passed the company continually attempted to improve both the quality of its products and the attractiveness of its packaging.

Over the decades, some product lines have been discontinued, such as those for foot or athletic uses, and digestive aides. Sometimes a product was dropped when a competitor developed a line that dominated the market.

A one-shot product during World War II and the Korean War was a gas mask to be used by civilians, if the need arose. It never did. The masks were made at the request of the federal government.

Sine-Aid was created by J&J as a product that was efficient and free of the antihistimine ingredient contained in many cold tablets. Its name was selected because it sounds like Band-Aid. No J&J corporate name was used on the package because "Johnson means pure" and, at least in sinus headache cures, that means ineffective.

Levi Strauss and Co.

"Yep. Pants don't wear worth a hoot up in the diggins. You can't get a pair strong enough to last no time."
Miner Speaking in 1850

Like so many other developments, Levi's were born in wartime. In 1850, Levi Strauss (1829-1902)* migrated to San Francisco. Drawn by Gold Rush

*When Strauss died in 1902, the San Francisco Call devoted a full-sized picture plus three front page columns to his obituary. One of the headlines read: "His Life Devoted Not Only to Fostering the Highest Commercial Conditions, But to the Moral, Social and Educational Welfare and Development of the Young Men and Women of the State."

Fig. 51. *Levi Strauss.* Founder Levi Strauss was only 17 years old when he came to New York from Bavaria. He spent his first years in America working for his two brothers peddling clothes and household items. Six years later, spurred on by exciting tales of instant wealth in the Gold Rush, he came to California. The "gold" he found was not in the hills, but rather in the sturdy and durable pair of pants he created which still bear his name today: Levi's jeans.
Courtesy, *Levi Strauss and Co.*

fever, he was a twenty-two-year-old German immigrant seeking to make his mark selling silks, broadcloths and fine dress goods to the miners. He also took with him a large supply of canvas duck for tents and Conestoga wagon covers.

On the long voyage around Cape Horn, the other passengers purchased everything but the canvas duck. When Strauss landed in California and spread out his stock, only one miner took the time to look it over and then, wagging his head, said that he should have brought pants to sell. What was urgently needed in frontier California was strong, durable pants.

Levi Strauss promptly headed for the nearest tailor, a roll of canvas under his arm. He had the canvas made into pants and soon visitors from the diggings would be asking where they could find "those pants of Levi's." Soon, his stock of canvas dwindled and he started to use local stocks of sailcloth. Dispatching letters to his relatives in New York, Levi asked them to ship all available heavy cloth. They responded with a generous variety, out of which he selected a heavy cotton of French origin, "serge de Nimes." Soon this name became "denim." Later, Levi selected a special shade of indigo blue dye for the material that made the pants that carried his "two horse brand" label (see below).

In the 1860's, Jacob W. Davis, a tailor in Carson City, Nevada, began riveting the pocket corners on miner's pants for added strength. Strauss liked the idea and together with Davis applied for a patent on strengthening Levi's overalls with copper rivets at all points of strain. The patent was granted in 1873 and the rivets stayed on Levi's jeans until 1937 when they were covered on back pockets because they were scratching saddles and school furniture. They were later replaced by stitched bar tackings.

Strauss introduced another innovation in 1873, the arcuate design. A double arc stitched on the back pockets with orange thread, it is known world-wide as the mark of authentic Levi's jeans and has been in use longer than any other apparel trademark in America. The word "bluejeans" written as one word first appeared around 1880.

In 1886 the famous two-horse guarantee patch, which depicts two horses straining to pull apart a pair of pants, was added as an additional identifying mark and like the arcuate is still used on a variety of Levi's apparel.

Custom fitting Levi's—low-hipped, snug and tapering at the legs—are the only item of wearing apparel whose style has remained basically the same for more than 127 years. Several pairs of Levi's jeans are part of the Smithsonian Institution's Americana Collection in Washington, D.C.

From the very beginning, Levi's had a host of imitators. Cowboys, lum-

Fig. 52. *Early Levi's Users.* Miners at the Virginia City Comstock Lode posed for their portraits over 100 years ago wearing Levi's jeans. Originally designed for the men who worked the California gold fields and Nevada silver mines, Levi's jeans have become so popular that today they are worn by people from every walk of life and have spread to world-wide fame.

Courtesy, *Levi Strauss & Co.*

Fig. 53. *Levi's "Two Horse" Trademark.*

Courtesy, *Levi Strauss & Co.*

berjacks, farmers, miners and students who, over the years, have depended on the quality of Levi's, have learned to look for the two-horse brand label and the back pocket tab that guaranteed they were getting authentic Levi's products. The fact that so many manufacturers, both here and abroad, try to duplicate Levi's styling is prime evidence of the high regard in which the company and its products are held.

In contrast to the rest of the apparel industry, Levi's did not always strive to be first with the newest. Instead, it led with what was the best. Over the years the company concentrated on expanding the line of garments. Children's Koveralls, Lady's Levi's, Western style shirts, jackets and riding pants were included in the expanding production.

In the 1930's many Western ranches converted into vacation hotels for wealthy Eastern vacationers who delighted in dressing up like cowboys. Dude ranches flourished and the guests greatly enjoyed taking their new western garb home with them, introducing Levi's for the first time east of the Mississippi.

During World War II, Levi's were declared an essential commodity and were sold only to people engaged in defense work. Following the war there was such an overwhelming demand for Levi's that deliveries had to be rationed for almost two years. In the early 1950's production facilities were expanded and the company began to catch up with demand. Levi's also entered the men's casual slacks field.

In the 1960's, Levi's introduced tan cotton twill pants, fashioned along the same lines as the original blue jeans. Teenagers soon named them White Levi's and the name stuck, even though the garment has since been made available in a variety of colors and fabrics.

Stretch Levi's were introduced in 1963 and one year later the company produced StaPrest, a process that revolutionized the apparel industry and the first real permanent press in the field.

The company has never stopped growing and it is constantly expanding the lines, pioneering with new fabrics, styles and colors.

In 1972 belts were added to the product lines and in 1975 Levi's for Feet, originally introduced in Australia several years ago, were offered to the American consumer for the first time. Ski Levi's is one of the newest lines, along with Levi's Socks.

Today, Levi Strauss & Co. is the largest apparel manufacturer in the world, and the largest manufacturer of men's suits, totaling $1.2 billion in yearly sales. It is a company that produces the most favored brand of leisure wear for every member of the family, both in the U.S. and abroad.

Walter Baker Chocolate Co. (General Foods)

"In Bishopsgate Street, in Queen's Head Alley, at a Frenchmen's house, is an excellent West Indies drink called Chocolate to be sold, where you may have it ready at any time, and also unmade at reasonable rates"

Publick Adviser,
June 16-22, 1657

The story of Walter Baker Chocolate begins with Dr. James Baker of Dorchester, Massachusetts. One day, in the fall of 1764, the doctor befriended a young Irish immigrant by the name of John Hannon. A chocolate maker by trade, Hannon lamented the fact that no none had yet had the initiative to set up a chocolate mill in the New World.

The doctor decided to help Hannon. He knew that James Boies' new mill on the Neponset River, in the heart of Dorchester, could be leased. He supplied the capital to get started, and together Baker and Hannon obtained a run of mill stones and a set of kettles. Early in 1765, the mill started production. The business has continued ever since.

The new industry prospered. But then, just when everything was run-

131

ning smoothly, misfortune struck. In 1779, John Hannon started off for the West Indies to purchase cocoa beans, but he never reached his destination. Though he was presumed lost at sea, what actually happened is still a mystery.

The following year, Dr. Baker acquired full ownership of the plant and began making a blend of quality chocolate which he called Baker's.

The mill continued as a family business for over 100 years. In 1791, Dr. Baker took his son Edmund into the partnership, and 13 years later he retired. Walter Baker, who was Edmund's son, became a partner in 1818. When Edmund retired six years later, Walter gave the company the name by which its products have since been known.

After Walter Baker's death, the company was run by his brother-in-law, Sidney Williams, and when he passed away, it was leased and finally sold to Henry L. Pierce, a nephew of Walter Baker. The company was incorporated in 1895 as Walter Baker and Company, Ltd. In 1927 it became a part of General Foods.

From its infancy, the company has been a consistent advertiser. As early as 1777, Hannon was publishing a moneyback, satisfaction guarantee. Abraham Lincoln and his partner, William Barry, sold Walter Baker's Breakfast Cocoa in their store in New Salem, Illinois, in 1833—the only packaged and advertised food product they carried. Advertising, quality products and the

Fig. 54. *La Belle Chocolatiere.*
Courtesy, *Walter Landor Museum of Packaging Antiquities*

132

charming "La Belle Chocolatiere" have made the Walter Baker name and products familiar to generations of housewives.

There's an interesting story in "La Belle Chocolatiere," Walter Baker's famous trademark (used since 1825). Twenty years before Hannon's mill was started, young Prince Ditrichstein, an Austrian nobleman, ventured into one of Vienna's quaint chocolate shops to try the new beverage introduced from the western tropics. He enjoyed the beverage, but for him a far more important discovery was Anna Baltauf, a waitress at the chocolate shop and daughter of Melchior, an impoverished knight. The Prince fell in love with her, and later that year they married.

As a wedding gift the Prince had his bride's portrait drawn in pastel by Jean Etienne Liotard, a famous Swiss portrait painter. Liotard posed her in the chocolate server's dress she wore the day she met her husband-to-be. Today her picture, "La Belle Chocolatiere," is one of the world's best known portraits and trademarks. The original hangs in the Dresden Gallery in Germany.

While this story is certainly a charming one, there is another version. Jean Etienne Liotard was in Vienna around 1742 to do the portraits of the Imperial family. (He had just come back from a trip with Lord Duncannon to Constantinople and had, in colorful fashion, adopted the Oriental costume—they called him in Vienna "the Turkish painter.")

Walter Baker's German Sweet Chocolate includes the use of another surname whose connotation is quite misleading. The man who worked with Walter Baker in the development of this sweet chocolate and who was rewarded with a spot in the trade name was his coachman, a man named German. He was an Englishman.

La Belle Chocolatiere turned up on a stamp from the Red Zone of Germany. The stamp—one of a series of six depicting the works of well-known European masters—was issued in late '55 to publicize the return of famous art works to the Dresden Art Gallery. During World War II, all pictures in the Dresden collection were removed for safety, and nothing was heard of them until recently.

Morton's Salt

"When It Rains It Pours"
Anon.

The story behind the famous Morton Salt trademark began about 1910, when the Morton Salt Company was organized from the merger of several smaller firms. Most dealers were then purchasing 300-pound barrels of salt

Fig. 55. *Growth of the Morton Salt Girl.* Evolution of Morton Salt packaging (left to right). Upper row: 1914, 1921, 1933; lower row: 1941, 1956, 1968.

Courtesy, *Morton Salt,* a division of *MortonNorwich*

and dispensing smaller amounts to their retail customers. Efforts to get these dealers to buy three- or five-pound boxes of salt had met with minimal success. Morton's "Seal Salt," a high-grade table salt packed in a paper-lined bag, also had failed to meet with consumer approval. To again attempt to capture the imagination of the consumer, Joy Morton turned his attention to a new, free-running salt, which he packed in a spouted, round package. In 1912 Morton's Table Salt was launched in the blue-and-white, asphalt-laminated paper cannister with an aluminum pouring spout. This carton, invented by J. R. Harbeck, was eventually adopted as the standard for the entire salt industry.

The Morton Salt Company decided to advertise on a national scale, and

134

in 1911 the little Umbrella Girl became a part of American commercial history.

The selection of the trademark was made by Sterling Morton II, then president of the company:

> One of the agency men suggested we might look at the three substitutes to see if we liked any of them better than the twelve which the agency considered best. I was immediately struck with one of the three. It showed a little girl standing in the rain with an umbrella over her head; under one arm she had a package of salt tilted backward with the spout open, and the salt running out. It struck me that here was the whole story in one picture. The message we wanted to put across—that the salt would run in damp weather—was made beautifully evident. I knew immediately that we could find no better trademark.
>
> Under the drawing of the little girl was the legend, "Even in rainy weather it flows freely." This struck me as being pretty good but rather on the long side. I distinctly remember saying that what we needed was something short and snappy like "Ivory Soap - It Floats." We worked around with "Flows freely, runs freely," but none seemed quite right. Finally, the word "pours" was suggested. That filled the bill, so "It Pours" as well as the words "Free Running" were approved for the new label.
>
> Then history was made. Someone (and I wish I knew who!) said, "There is an old proverb, It never rains but it pours." I think everyone in the room realized that we had something there. After a little discussion, I suggested that "never" and "but" struck me as poor words to use, that negative connotations should be avoided in a slogan, so we then turned the old proverb around and made it positive instead of negative—When It Rains It Pours. We knew that was it and our famous trademark and slogan were launched on their triumphant career.

Gerber Baby Foods

"America's best-known baby."
The Gerber Baby Foods
Trademark

To mothers shopping in a supermarket the display of baby food is a familiar sight. But it wasn't that long ago that mothers had to strain fruits and vegetables by hand. The Gerbers changed all that.

The Gerber story begins in a small town—Fremont, Michigan—in timberland country. The land was cleared at the turn of the century to cultivate the soil, which was very fertile. Shortly thereafter a small cannery was formed to provide a steady market for local produce. The Fremont Cannery was formed. Frank Gerber was asked to take charge of the new company. Mr. Ger-

135

ber's family had settled in the area originally because of his keen interest in the lumber industry. Frank Gerber knew this part of the country well and was fully aware of the need for a processing industry in Fremont. Thanks to his industriousness and sharp business acumen, the small cannery grew and prospered. By 1928, it was a well-established company in the United States, known for its quality canned fruits and vegetables. In 1928, a major change occurred in the company. Dan Gerber, Frank's son, precipitated that change.

Dan Gerber was a young married man with a small baby in 1928. The Gerber's pediatrician suggested that the young Gerber baby be switched from his liquid diet, used during most of the first year, to solid foods—of course, all strained. This was a formidable chore as well as frustrating and time consuming, as Dan Gerber watched his wife struggle with assorted straining utensils and a can of Fremont peas. The next day at the company Dan Gerber asked his father, Frank, if he thought mothers around the country would welcome a line of commercially prepared baby food. Dan got the approval of his father and the Gerber production line was soon producing some sample batches of strained fruits and vegetables. A panel of babies was brought in to test the samples, and they met with the babies lip-smacking approval. This was translated to "better than home-prepared." The reason for the excellent taste of these baby foods was that the plant could obtain fresher produce than was available at the stores and that the quick commercial straining and cooking excluded enough air to make a noticeable differ-

Fig. 56. *Daniel F. Gerber.*
Courtesy, *Gerber Products Co.*

136

ence in flavor. After consultation with pediatricians and specialists, the Gerbers were ready to market their new product, but first a survey was taken to see if this unusual product would be accepted. The survey offered positive results and Dan Gerber was ready to go ahead with his advertising campaign to introduce the product to mothers all over the United States. The advertising budget was limited and the advertisements would have to be small. Dan thought it would be a good idea to include an illustration of a healthy, happy baby as a quick attention-getter. The whole world loves a happy beautiful baby, thought Dan Gerber. He was right!

Many paintings, illustrations and sketches of babies were submitted to the Fremont company for review. A sketch in charcoal by artist Dorothy Hope Smith was accepted by the judges unanimously. The baby was beautiful and rosy-cheeked and just the right age, too. This baby illustration became an official trademark.* Surveys would show that it was "America's best-known baby." Reprints of it would be in constant demand. Following a modest advertisement featuring the Gerber baby trademark, the product won immediate public acceptance. Within six months the product was on the shelves of grocery stores in most major areas, and was known as Gerber Baby Foods. From this point on the company enjoyed a steady growth. Gerber Products Company today is the only leading manufacturer that exclusively produces specialized baby foods. The Gerber people are proud of the fact that "Babies are our business . . . . our only business!"

Fig. 57. *The Gerber Baby.* Copyright, Gerber Products Company. Courtesy, *Gerber Products Co.*

*The sketch was completed in 1928. The artist indicated that she would complete it if the age and size of the baby were approved. The sketch was so appealing that the artist's unfinished rendering became the world-famous trademark. The original drawing is kept under glass in the company vault.

Spalding Sporting Goods

"Spalding has gone into the baseball business."
Spalding Co. sign (1876)

Albert Goodwill Spalding began his work career as a failure in business. Within a period of five years he worked for five different firms—all of them failed soon after his arrival. He felt jinxed as a businessman and returned to his first love, baseball.

In 1871, Spalding became a pitcher-outfielder for the Boston Red Stockings and then pitched for the Chicago White Sox. In his first season with the Boston Red Stockings, he pitched his team to a pennant victory. During his career he won a total of 241 games.

After only four years as a baseball player, Spalding decided he would like to return to business—but this time as a baseball hero. (He made the baseball Hall of Fame and was the sport's first 200-game winner). In March, 1876, he opened up his Sporting Goods Emporium in Chicago. The sign on his Emporium stated "Spalding has gone into the baseball business." He promoted his own baseball, which he had invented for his own use as a player. Spalding baseball was proclaimed the offficial ball for league use by the National Baseball League and sales took off after that. In the late 1880's the hub of the manufacturing industry was Chicopee, Massachusetts. A. G. Spalding Sporting Goods Company thought it judicious to be part of that hub and soon moved to Chicopee, where Spalding expanded his line to include baseball equipment, the first U.S. made tennis balls and footballs and a new Spalding designed tennis racket. In 1891 James Naismith devised a game called "Basketball."* The ball he used was a common soccer ball, but as the game quickly became a sensation, it was only natural that the basketball people should want their own ball (see Table 8.2). It was just as natural for Dr. Naismith to seek assistance from the already prominent sporting goods company in nearby Chicopee, Massachusetts. The result? A new Spalding designed ball was soon in production and the official rules of the game of basketball compiled in 1901 state, "The ball made by A. G. Spalding Brothers shall be the official ball."

Another first in the United States sporting industry was golf clubs, introduced by Albert Spalding in 1894. In the world of sporting goods Spalding had built up a reputation for the finest quality produced in the United States. Thus Spalding products became the official choice of various organizations

---

*Basketball was introduced in Great Britain in 1893 by Madame Bergman-Osterberg at Hampstead Physical Training College.

TABLE 8.2

EVOLUTION OF THE BASKETBALL

Date	Development
1894	Original Leather Basketball
1926	First Laceless Basketball
1935	Improved Laceless Basketball
1937	Original "Last Bilt" (bonding leather panels)
1976	Official Olympic Ball

and leagues.

Spalding deems it essential to custom design their sporting goods to receive the personal endorsements (in return for a fee) of famous players in every sport. For example, Spalding designs a special baseball glove for each of the six player positions, and also in a Professional, Collegiate, Youth and Youngstar series, as well. Every one of these gloves has the personal endorsement, with the signature of a baseball superstar.

To maintain its image of high quality sporting goods, Spalding employs a Sports Advisory Staff of more than 250 athletes who are given substantial fees to use and evaluate the equipment and offer suggestions to make improvements when necessary. Sometimes the star is the originator of a new piece of equipment.

Spalding also keeps a good working relationship with top playing professionals and top teachers in all its chosen fields.

The Spalding company cultivates many markets. The Spalding name is sold mainly through retail sporting goods dealers and through professional shops. But Spalding feels it most important for company growth to reach a larger market area, so the company developed a special product line to reach discount stores and private brand sellers as well as premium and incentive operations.

Thus the evolution of the A. G. Spalding Company began with Albert's baseball (of his own making)—which he used to achieve an amazing single season record of 47 wins and 14 losses—and grew to cover every single sport in which balls are used in the United States, including the little pink ball used for such street games as Captain and hit the penny, as well as baseball gloves, tennis rackets and golf clubs.

Hershey Chocolate Corp.

"He worked it all out for himself. Milton did every-
thing the hard-way. No short-cuts."
Milton Hershey's formula for
milk chocolate (as told by an
associate ca. 1915)

Milton Snavely Hershey was born in poverty in 1857 on a farm in Pennsylvania Dutch country in Lancaster, Pa. He was the son of Henry Hershey
and Fanny Snavely Hershey and the lineal descendant of Andrew Hershey, a
bishop in the Mennonite church. Andrew Hershey came from Switzerland in
1719 to settle in Pennsylvania.

Milton had a harsh childhood. His father Henry went bankrupt while
Milton was quite young and the family was forced to move to smaller quarters
on his uncle's farm, where he was given the responsibility of maintaining the
farm, which included endless chores. He attended school when he could get
there—the school was two miles away and was just a tiny schoolhouse. But he
did learn the 3 R's and at fourteen became a printer's apprentice. He had no
aptitude for printing, however, and it was decided that he learn another
trade. Since Royess Confectionary store was nearby and was training young
boys at the time, he joined the training program and at nineteen became a
full-fledged journeyman. He soon set out on his own, opening up a small
kitchen in Philadelphia where he made penny candies. He was a success and
his business grew. He would make the candies by night and sell them by day.
This rigorous schedule wore him down and finally broke his health. His life
hung in the balance and so did his candy business. With the constant care and
devotion of his beloved Mother he returned to health and to his candy-
making venture. In his seventh year in Philadelphia, Hershey expanded his
business to the wholesale trade. Sales were excellent but the sugar refineries
demanded immediate cash for the sugar he bought. He was unable to meet
their demands and soon was forced to sell his business.

Milton decided to try his luck in another big city—Chicago—manufacturing caramels in a small basement at night and selling them to street ven-
dors in the daytime. He was doing well when his father lured him to Denver
by writing that there was a need for a good candy business there. After closing
his business in Chicago and moving to Denver, he soon realized that this need
resulted from the wishful thinking and false hopes of his father. He went back
to Lancaster as a broken and unhappy man. However, this did not deter
Milton from starting out all over again. This time it was New York City, where
he opened a small factory with some money saved from his Philadelphia busi-

140

ness and some additional money from his Aunt. His specialty—caramels. His secret to success this time was the fresh milk in the caramels, which gave them a unique, creamy taste. Milton's business boomed and he hired cooks to prepare his candy recipe while he went out to solicit business. The combination of being a super salesperson and having an excellent product proved quite lucrative. He expanded and hired more help. But again bad luck followed him to New York. An unfortunate error on his part brought this business to a close. He inadvertently overstayed his lease at his old location by just a few days, but this did not stop his landlord from sueing him for an additional year's rent. Since he was unable to meet the obligation of a double rent he

TABLE 8.3

HERSHEY HIGHLIGHTS

Date	Product
1894	The Hershey Bar and Almond Bar, Hershey's Cocoa, Hershey's Baking Chocolate
1907	Hershey's Kisses*
1923	Reese's Peanut Butter Cups, Y & S Nibs
1925	Mr. Goodbar
1926	Hershey's Syrup
1928	Y & S Twizzlers
1938	Krackel
1939	Hershey's Miniatures
1940	Hershey's Hot Chocolate (now Hot Cocoa Mix)
1941	Dainties (now Semi-Sweet Chocolate Chips)
1952	Chocolate Fudge Topping
1956	Instant Cocoa Mix (Hershey's Instant)
1970	Kit Kat
1971	Special Dark
1976	Reese's Crunchy
1977	Reese's Peanut Butter Flavored Chips, Golden Almond
1978	Reese's Pieces, Giant Kiss
1979	Whatchamacallit

*July 1, 1907 – Introduction of Hershey's Kisses

August 8, 1921 – Identification plume (streamer) added to Hershey's Kisses

April 20, 1933 – "Kiss for You" label introduced (discontinued October 31, 1956)

September 1970 – First national consumer advertising program introduced

December 1978 – Introduction of 8 oz. Giant Kiss

141

was forced to close his doors for the third time.

He returned again to Lancaster and with the backing of his uncles embarked on his fourth candy business. Milton said this would be his last try at making a go of a business. After all, at age thirty-six he already had experienced three failures, enough to break the strongest will. He felt he had accumulated enough knowledge and business acumen to do it right this time, and he was right. When real success finally came, it was sudden and quite by chance. An English importer tasted Milton's special fresh milk recipe for caramels. He then gave him a large order. If this quality was maintained, said the importer, his next order would be even bigger. Hershey was well aware that fresh milk would be the key to his success, since it gave the caramel its unique flavor. This he learned from his candy-making experiences in Denver and New York. Within just a few years he was the owner of a large new caramel candy factory. The company grew to cover a city block within a few years after he opened its doors. Only once did he experience a setback. While Hershey was on the very first vacation in his life, his manager experimented with a substitute for fresh milk. The experiment was a disaster, causing a loss of sixty thousand dollars to the business. But this lesson drew his attention to the magic of fresh milk and, ultimately, to Milk Chocolate. But, where the caramel recipe was quite simple, the milk chocolate was quite complex.

Fig. 58. *Milton F. Hershey.*
Courtesy, *Hershey Foods Corp.*

142

Fig. 59. *Early Packaging Line. Employees weighing 2½* pound boxes of Hershey's
Kisses in the early 1920's.

Courtesy, *Hershey Foods Corp.*

Fig. 60. *Early Labeling Line.* Employee working at a labeling machine on Hershey's
Cocoa Can line in the early 1920's.

Courtesy, *Hershey Foods Corp.*

143

In 1893, Milton Hershey went to the Chicago Exposition. At the fair there was very intriguing chocolate-making machinery, the first of its kind. He immediately purchased this machinery and started experimenting with fresh milk and cocoa beans. What Hershey was looking for was an inexpensive manufacturing process. Up to this time, milk chocolate was sold in one or two pound boxes and was quite expensive—well out of reach of the average person.

In 1900, Milton Hershey sold his caramel candy business for $1,000,000, and went into his most successful venture—Hershey's Milk Chocolate. The cornerstone to his success was fine quality ingredients including fresh milk. Since he already was in cow country, fresh milk was in abundant supply.

The only way he could sell his chocolate to large numbers of people was to make it available in drugstores, food stores and candy stores, and at a cheap price. This required mass production. So, using the machinery he had purchased at the Chicago Exposition and the labor of reliable and honest local Mennonite employees, he produced a wrapped milk chocolate candy bar for five cents. In 1900 no such product existed. Bold distribution to reach large numbers of people was his next step. Hershey recruited a large sales force and gave them these instructions: "Put the Hershey Milk Chocolate Bar on every counter, shelf, stand and rack in every retail establishment in the United States—food store, restaurant, drug store, ice cream parlor and soda fountain." This mass availability was a revolutionary idea in 1900, but it worked!

In 1903, ground was broken for the first large building of the Hershey Chocolate Company. This was a series of limestone buildings that eventually would cover six acres.

In 1907, the famous Hershey Chocolate Kiss was introduced. Its slogan was "A kiss for you." The milk chocolate recipe for the "kiss" contains sugar, milk, cocoa butter and chocolate, with soya licithin (an emulsifier) and vanillin flavoring. This milk chocolate recipe worked out by Hershey was used to produce the beautifully shaped Hershey kiss. The wrapped Kiss configuration is a registered trademark of Hershey Food Corporation. The plant is the largest chocolate factory in the United States today. It is also one of the largest industries of its kind in the world.

Milton Hershey was a generous man. When beginning his Milk Chocolate Manufacturing business he said "I am not going into the chocolate business to add to my wealth. I have all the money I need. What I want to do is to put it to work so that it will benefit others." He endowed the Milton Hershey school for orphans with the majority stock ownership in the company. This is just one of the many contributions he has given to the people of "Hershey" town in what is now known as Hershey, Pennsylvania.

Twining Tea (associated British Foods Group)

*"That Excellent, and by all Physitians approved
China Drink called by the Chineans Teha, by other
nations Tay, alias Tee, sold at the Sultanesshead, a
cophee house in Sweetings Rents by the Royal Exchange in London"*.

First Advertisement for Tea
in England (1658)

The history of tea is a colorful one, starting with an old Chinese legend
that the tea-plant sprang to life after Buddha, whilst meditating under a bo-
tree, cut off his eyelids and flung them to the ground in order to stay awake.
But the true origins of tea started for much more practical reasons. For health,
the Chinese used to boil water for drinking but this left the water with a nasty
taste, so they began the practice of adding herbs to the water to give it a more
palatable flavor.

The first printed mention of tea in Europe, however, did not occur until
the middle of the 16th century. Thereafter, most explorers, sailors and traders
brought back many and varied stories about the tea plant and the exciting
drink that could be made from it. Tea was soon regarded as having strong
medicinal qualities, which rapidly increased its popularity. By the mid-1650's
tea was being sold in Holland, but mainly through the apothecaries. A few
years later, it also became available in this country through colonial
warehouses—the equivalent of the modern grocer.

In 1664, the East India Company placed an order for a single consign-
ment of tea with their Far Eastern agents. The same year, when one of the
company's fleet returned from Bantam a small parcel of 'thea' was presented,
among other gifts, to Charles II. This helped to launch tea as a fashionable
court drink, and from then on, it became more and more popular among the
English.

During this period coffee houses were being opened all over London;
but a greedy government levied taxes on certain beverages served in these
popular meeting places.

THE BEGINNINGS OF TWINING TEA

The will of Thomas Rashleigh Esquire of Blackheath, Kent, dated February 1, 1830, bequeathed "to Mrs. Perry, mother of my two female servants,
my two brown china jars in my study filled with tea from Twinings such as I
drink myself." The recipient of this bequest must surely have thought herself

fortunate since in the early years of the nineteenth century, fine tea was still a costly luxury. By 1837, when Queen Victoria granted a Royal Warrant to Richard Twining II "as Purveyor of Tea in Ordinary to Her Majesty," the long monopoly of the East India Company had been broken, and the price of tea had begun to come down within the reach of others than the aristocracy and royalty.

The house of Twining was established in 1706, when Thomas Twining (1675–1741), a freeman of the city of London, opened Master Tom's Coffee House at the sign of the Golden Lion on the Strand. After arriving in London from the West Country at the age of ten, Twining was apprenticed to a weaver in order to become a freeman, a necessary qualification for those who conducted trade in the city. He attained freeman's status in 1703 and went into the employ of Thomas D'Aeth, wealthy East India merchant, from whom he learned about tea.

When Thomas Twining opened his coffeehouse, there were already well over a thousand such establishments, each catering to a special group. Into this fierce competition came Thomas Twining with his specialty: tea. Tea was viewed as an exotic beverage and was extolled by its supporters as a cure-all. On the other hand, it was denounced as wicked by the clergy, who termed it "a base unworthy Indian practice," and by the brewers, who were afraid it would replace ale at breakfast. It was also heavily taxed, so that a pound of the cheapest tea would cost about a third of a skilled worker's weekly salary at the time.

By 1717, Thomas Twining found it necessary to enlarge his operation to cope with greatly increased business. His reputation as a tea blender and merchant had spread and tea now accounted for the largest part of his business. In addition to selling dry tea to his customers, he began to supply a number of coffeehouses and nearby inns.

Thomas Twining was followed into business by his son Daniel, whose premature death in 1762 led to the company being taken over by his widow, Mary Little, who had two young children. She ran it for twenty years, a considerable achievement for a woman in the eighteenth-century man's world. When her son Richard completed his education, she taught him the art of tea blending and the intricacies of the tea trade.

Richard took the reins in 1783 and quickly settled into the business. So much so that just a year later, in his capacity as Chairman of the Dealers of Tea, he persuaded William Pitt to reduce the very high tax on tea. The Commutation Act, by reducing the price, made tea more accessible to the general public. Without this important change in fiscal law, it is unlikely that the British would be a nation of tea drinkers today.

Until 1838, when the first shipment of Assam tea from India was brought to London by the tea clipper Calcutta, only China tea had been available. The Chinese were most secretive about their tea and had not permitted seeds or seedlings to be exported. But tea had been discovered growing wild in India, and with the blessings of the government, widescale cultivation had successfully begun. A healthy trade with India was soon established, with the famous tea clippers like the Cutty Sark transporting the now-popular Indian tea to England. In 1875, the first small shipments of tea from Ceylon began to arrive. By 1880, Ceylon tea had become well established, giving England a range of three major sources for tea.

Richard Twining was followed into the business by his son, Richard II, who was responsible for the establishment of Twinings Bank at number 215 Strand next door to the tea company. The handsome new building was much remarked by the press when it opened for business in 1836. In 1892, this bank was merged with Lloyds Bank, becoming known as Lloyds Bank, Twinings Branch. Several members of the Twining family subsequently became officers of Lloyds.

Richard II served as head of the firm from 1818 to 1857, when he died at the age of eighty-five. By the time Richard III took over as head of the firm in 1857, the coffeehouses were but a memory and the tea gardens, which had followed them in popularity, had disappeared as a growing London engulfed them. Richard III served as head of the firm until 1897, when he retired, and after the turn of the century, new generations of Twinings took over the firm.

Twinings continued to blend tea to individual customer's specifications into the 1930's, but changes brought about in the pace of life by the automobile and World War I led Twinings into the production of pre-packaged blends. Today, in their 275th anniversary year, Twinings continues to produce a range of nineteen different tea blends. All are available in the traditional tins; thirteen are also available as tea bags.

The original Twinings shop on the Strand in London is today a museum, but continues to sell the special blends that made Twinings a famous Victorian drink.

Gillette Razors

On one particular morning when I started to shave, I found my razor dull, and it was not only dull but it was beyond the point of successful stropping and it needed honing, for which it must be taken to a barber or to a cutler. As I stood there with the razor in

147

> *my hand, my eyes resting on it as lightly as a bird*
> *settling down on its nest—the Gillette razor was*
> *born.*
>
> King C. Gillette (1920)

Changing the face of man—his image and his habits—is certainly a broad statement to make, but that is just what happened when King C. Gillette invented the first disposable safety razor in the summer of 1895. In just a few short years after his invention, men around the world were shaving off their beards. Before the safety razor was invented, shaving was a tedious, difficult and time-consuming task, which most men would struggle through about twice a week. A straight-edge-hook-type razor was used in the nineteenth century. The five o'clock shadow was a curse yet undreamed of, and most men up to the turn of the century agreed with this old Russian proverb, "It is easier to bear a child once a year than to shave every day." Only the rich who could afford a barber shaved every day and that too had its disadvantages, since many barbers of the eighteenth and nineteenth centuries were not always clean and one would have to put up with dirty fingers and bad breath, as well as with the procedure of blood letting. Benjamin Franklin documented this when he said, "I reckon it among my felicities that I can set my own razor and shave myself perfectly well in which I have a daily pleasure and avoid the uneasiness one is sometimes obliged to suffer from the dirty fingers and bad breath of a slovenly barber." Unfortunately, most men did not acquire the skill and patience that was required for shaving, especially on a daily basis. Before the safety razor, it was necessary to maintain the blades, which needed stropping before each use and after a month or so needed honing in the hands of an expert cutler. Cutting oneself while shaving was a very common occurrence until Gillette's safety razor came along.

Who was this man who revolutionized shaving?

The Gillette family can trace its American origins to Nathan Gillet, one of two brothers who came to Massachusetts on the ship Mary and John in the year 1630. The Gillets were sons of the Reverend William Gillet of Chaffcombe, Somerset, England. King Gillette was born in Fond du Lac, Wisconsin in 1855. His father George Gillette was a sometime postmaster, inventer-tinkerer and weekly newspaper editor. His mother Fanny Lemira Camp also came from early colonial stock. There is a pre-revolutionary house known as the Camp House which still stands in Salisbury, Connecticut. Fanny Camp was a strong disciplinarian although she was known as kind and, according to King, never uttered a harsh word. However, she demanded near perfection in her children. Because of her insistence on perfection and organization, she is considered to be a great influence on the lifestyle of her son

148

Fig. 61. *King C. Gillette.*

Courtesy, *The Gillette Co.*

King, who developed a life-long belief in efficiency and never wasting time. In the 1860's, King Gillette's father promoted a shingle-making machine and worked as a patent agent. King's parents' philosophy for their children was never let the children be idle, and thus they were encouraged to work with their hands, to figure out how things work and to ask questions. According to King Gillette, they were a close, self-sufficient family "knit together by close bonds of affection and mutual interest." Although the family was self-sufficient, close knit and inventive, they could not avoid the ravages of the Chicago fire in October 1871, which wiped out King Gillette's father's business. So the family pulled up stakes and moved to a city of greater

149

opportunity—New York, where George Gillette set up a hardware supply business. Meanwhile seventeen-year-old King Gillette decided to strike out on his own. At first he began clerking in various wholesale hardware houses. By the age of twenty-one he was a traveling salesman. What made King Gillette different from his colleagues in the same business was his keen interest in tinkering with the metal products he sold, making them work better, expanding on a product and finally inventing some. In 1879, he patented a combination bushing and valve for water taps and a few years later took out another patent for a refined version of the same product. In 1889, he was granted another patent for inventing two types of conduits for electrical cables. Unfortunately, he did not make much money on these inventions because he never had time to promote them. He was too busy trying to make a living peddling his wares, and was a star salesman! Marriage and a new job were now on the agenda for King Gillette. He married Atlanta Ella Gaines, the daughter of a prosperous Ohio oilman, in 1889 and joined the Baltimore Seal Company in 1891. Upon joining the company, he formed a close friendship with the President of Baltimore Seal, William Painter, a successful inventor who said something to King Gillette that he would remember and that would inspire him to look for a unique invention. Painter said, "You are always thinking and inventing something. Why don't you try to think of something like the Crown Cork which, when once used, is thrown away, and the customer keeps coming back for more—and with every additional customer you get, you are building a foundation of profit." Painter's words became an obsession and Gillette began his search for a "throw away" something. But before he invented another item he felt compelled to write a book about society and how it should be structured for the future. After accomplishing this undertaking in 1894 and arranging for the book's national publication (the book was entitled *The Human Drift* to underscore his belief that the natural human tendency is toward ever greater centralization), Gillette began to think about his next invention.

He explained the dawn of his invention in great detail in his writings.

"On one particular morning when I started to shave" he wrote, "I found my razor dull, and it was not only dull but it was beyond the point of successful stropping and it needed honing, for which it must be taken to a barber or a cutler. As I stood there with the razor in my hand, my eyes resting on it as lightly as a bird settling down on its nest—the Gillette razor was born. I saw it all in a moment, and in that same moment many unvoiced questions were asked and answered more with rapidity of a dream than by the slow process of reasoning." He wrote to his wife who was visiting relatives in Ohio, "I've got it; our fortune is made." He knew this idea would revolutionize the

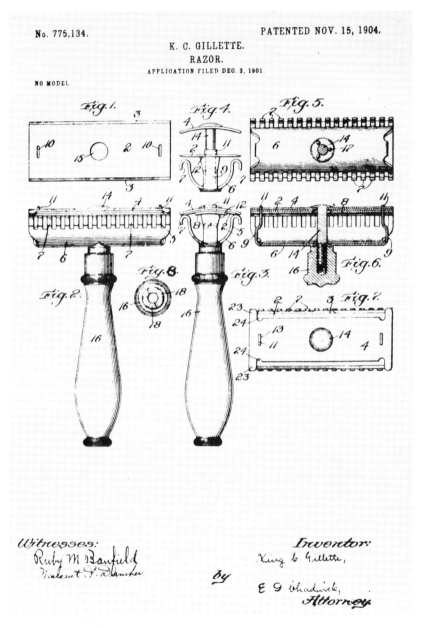

Fig. 62. *Early Gillette Patent.*

Courtesy, *The Gillette Co.*

process of shaving and he explains it this way: "The thought occurred to me that no radical improvement had been made in razors, especially in razor blades, for several centuries, and it flashed through my mind that if by any possibility razor blades could be constructed and made cheap enough to do away with honing and stropping and permit the user to replace dull blades by new ones, such improvements would be highly important in that art."

However, it took eight years and required the technical help of William Nickerson, a graduate of M.I.T., to perfect the safety razor and then get it on the market. This was a very lengthy testing time and Gillette wrote, "If I had been technically trained, I would have quit. But I was a dreamer, I didn't know enough to quit."

In the first year of marketing—1903—the Gillette Safety Razor Company sold 51 razors and 168 blades. But during its second year, it sold 90,884 razors and 123,648 blades. In 1904, the Gillette Company was awarded a U.S. patent on the razor. In its third year razor sales were rising 400 percent and blade sales were booming at a thousand percent. In that year the company opened its first overseas branch in London. King Gillette then began to feel that the company needed its own special identification, since it was now realizing a handsome profit and would, he thought, be in business for many years. Thus the company decided it should have a trademark with worldwide identification. The management felt the trademark should be as easily recognized as a U.S. dollar bill, with its portrait of George Washington. King Gillette was considered to be a distinguished and handsome man in his time, with his neatly turned mustache and his thick wavy black hair. Thus he was unanimously chosen to have his picture on every razor and blade package.

King Gillette retired in 1918 and went to California, but he retained the title of President of his company until 1931. The company he founded grew to about $1.5 billion in annual sales, with over 35 thousand employees.

King C. Gillette not only made his name as familiar as his invention, but also made his face familiar to millions of people. The blade wrapper with his picture was reproduced more than 100 billion times. This is considered to be the broadest personal publicity ever given to a businessman in the entire history of world commerce.

9
FAMOUS FEMALE
TRADEMARKS

Many advertisers have attempted to harness the po-
tentialities of pretty girls in their trademarks, gener-
ally with mediocre results. For a variety of technical
reasons, pretty girls have proved to be slippery crea-
tures that don't harness easily. One difficulty is in
the style of clothes, which may have to be modified
every year or two to keep the poor creature from
turning into a frump. An even greater difficulty
arises from the inconsistency of public tastes in the
ideal female.

Frank Rowsome, Jr. in
They Laughed When I
Sat Down (1959)

Although it might appear to be a natural trademark subject, women
have not been the feature of many common trademarks.* Problems with style
updating, aging and relation to current public tastes in the ideal female have
all plagued the trademark designer. Instead of a Betty Crocker or an Ann
Page, female trademarks have often taken the form of a historical or fictional
character such as Pocahontas, Queen Victoria, the goosegirl in a painting that
became Old Dutch Cleanser, Venus, the St. Pauli Girl or a busty and
bunting-draped Columbia. Not only are the latter safe and unchanging, but
they also do not represent a threat to the everyday shopper. One such example
in use today is the famous Humphrey's trademark. Used on the company's
complete line of homeopathic medicines, the trademark is an allegorical representation of a pretty girl running through a field. Her arms are outstretched

---

*One notable exception is "the Oxo Girl," who appeared in the U.K. in the 1930's. This near-
classic trademark depicted a six-year-old girl holding a steaming cup, and wrapped in a towel.
The girl was the daughter of Ernest Longmate, who used her as the model for his now-famous
illustrations.

TABLE 9.1

CIGARETTE BRAND TRADEMARKS

Nation	Brand	Type
U.K.	Lucky Dream	Seduction
U.K.	Gona	Seduction
U.K.	Island Queen	Seduction
China	Crab Beauty	Sexual
U.K.	Snake Charmer	Seduction
U.S.A.	Jezebel	Seduction
U.S.A.	Sin	Seduction
U.K.	Harem	Harem motif
U.K.	Crayol	Middle Eastern

and she resembles a Victorian beauty.

Over the years cigarette packages have often displayed beautiful and seductive women. This was part of the smoker's dream and she usually appeared in two forms—as a "femme fatale" or a "harem slave-girl" (see Table 9.1). Use of the white slave image was to emphasize the Turkish or Eastern type of cigarette. A rather interesting package is a 1930's Chinese product, Crab Beauty. On this pack, a seductive Chinese beauty is featured surrounded by a crab—a curious mixture of pleasure and pain.

Royalty, actresses and fictional female characters have also appeared as trademarks. Even though British Royal Family members do not allow direct references to themselves on packages for any product, there has been a Diamond Queen brand cigarettes (based on Queeen Victoria's Jubilee), Kroning's Sigarreten featuring a Queen of Holland's head and Jubilaum, which had a picture of King Christian IX and Queen Louisa of Denmark as its trademark.* There have also been Madame Butterfly and Winnie Winkle brand cigars on the market.

Women were also commonly used as trademarks for California oranges. In the early 1900's, it was assumed that women would be responding to trademark designs, and a majority of the trademarks on labels were rendered in soft colors depicting innocent women. When it was discovered that masculine appeal was needed (the fruit jobbers were usually male), the representation of the woman underwent a major transformation, constantly becoming more seductive. Trademarks of the 1940's and 50's were much along the lines of calendar pinup art—eventually featuring half-dressed women holding up

*Most of the packages using royalty as trademarks were based on commemoratives—marriages, jubilees and anniversaries.

154

TABLE 9.2

SOME FEMALE-CHARACTER TRADEMARKS

Brand	Product Line
Elizabeth Arden	Cosmetics
American Girl	Shoes
Mum (?)	Deodorant
General Foods' Baker's Brand Chocolate	Chocolate products
Aunt Jemima	Pancake mix
Venus de Milo	Face Cream
Virginia Dare	Vanilla
Fannie Farmer	Candies
Sophia	Perfume
Aunt Millie's	Tomato sauces

bunches of fruit.

Sozodont was the first large advertiser to use a female-character trademark. The Sozodont girl appeared in the 1880's as a woodcut and in the 1890's as a halftone. What started out as a handsome woman, ended up, years later, as a toothy portrait of a woman which threatened unruly children.

In spite of the above, there are several female-character trademarks in use today (see Table 9.2). Some are quite well known and contribute quite heavily toward their product sales. Others such as the smiling nurse (slightly outdated) on the carton of Hollywood brand shoe polish serve to reflect product quality to the consumer.

Betty Crocker

How do you make a one-crust cherry pie?
What's a good recipe for apple dumplings?
How long do you knead bread dough?
Questions sent to Betty
Crocker in the 1930s.

In 1921 the Wasburn Crosby Company, the forerunner of General Mills, used the name "Betty Crocker" in replies to homemakers' requests for recipes and help with baking problems. The surname was that of William G. Crocker, retiring director of the company's board. The name "Betty" was selected because it was popular at the time and was perceived to have a warm sound. In 1936, the first portrait of the corporate symbol was commissioned. The original Betty Crocker reflected the view of a 1930's housewife. She was a

155

Fig. 63. *Betty Crocker.* Second
Betty Crocker (1955).
Courtesy, *General Mills, Inc.*

homemaker in her mid-forties and dressed simply and frugally.

The 1980 model is the sixth Betty Crocker. In her mid-to-late thirties, she is about ten years younger than her predecessor, who was introduced in 1972. But like the others before her, Betty Crocker VI is a blue-eyed brunette. Her portrait, like all Betty Crockers, graces the cover of the new Betty Crocker Cookbook, and it will hang, as do those of her predecessors, in a hallway of the Betty Crocker test kitchens at the company headquarters, where 75,000 visitors tour each year. But her image will not be featured on General Mills packages. The image of Betty Crocker III was the last to be used for that. Still, 90 percent of the American public recognizes Betty Crocker today and relates her to General Mills.

Not everyone has responded warmly to Betty. In 1972, the National Organization of Women filed a class-action complaint charging General Mills with race and sex discrimination in perpetuating the image of Betty Crocker as a homemaker. Others, however, have been captivated by the Crocker image. Over the years, Betty Crocker has received hundreds of marriage proposals through the mail, apparently from men who believed she was real.

Psyche - The White Rock Girl

"What is the psychology of using a pretty face (in advertising)? The humblest that travels and reads will tell you that he is mysteriously inclined to regard the mechanical adjustment of the covered apparatus which hangs at the charming young woman's hip as being of a highly superior order of merit because of the beauty of face and raiment."

John Brisben Walker in
Cosmopolitan (1902)

Psyche has survived for more than 60 years, with only one major and a few minor overhauls. It all started at the 1893 World's Fair in Chicago when the owners of the White Rock Mineral Springs Company discovered a painting by Paul Thurman, a German artist, titled, "Psyche at Nature's Mirror." It showed a solid Teuton maiden, minimally garbed and just sprouting the wings that denoted her transition from girl to goddess. She was kneeling on a stone and peering at her reflection in a pool, presumably to see what deification was doing for her.

Psyche was Art Nouveau at its best. The use of a sensuous nymph coupled with a nature motif was characteristic of the then current artistic style. The White Rock people immediately bought rights to use the painting in advertising. First they incribed "White Rock" on the stone on which Psyche knelt. Then they made statues of her, put her on all their labels and extensively promoted her. For 31 years, Psyche survived almost untouched. In 1924, her hair style was changed to one then worn by Mary Pickford. In 1944, she was extensively rebuilt and modernized. Made taller, lighter and with an updated hairdo, she remained essentially unchanged until the 1970's. With women's liberation, her bra came off and she became the very embodiment of the modern woman. Yet to the trained eye, her very origin lies in the Art Nouveau movement of the 1890's.

Dolly Madison Ice Cream

Last night I was bid by our President to the White House (wrote a personality of the time), and it was a most unusual affair. Mrs. Madison always entertains with Grace and Charm, but last night there was a sparkle in her eye that set astir an Air of Expectancy among her Guests. When finally the brilliant Assemblage—America's best—entered the dining

157

> *room, they beheld a Table set with French china and*
> *English silver, laden with good things to eat, and in*
> *the centre high on a silver platter, a large shining*
> *dome of pink Ice Cream.*
>
> A Contemporary Account of a
> Dinner Given by Dolly Madison

Although ice cream was available in the United States as early as 1700, and both George Washington and Thomas Jefferson were known to be ice cream fanciers, President James Madison's wife, Dolly, is often credited with being the sole person responsible for making ice cream popular. From the expensive delicacy that it had been in the late eighteenth century, it became, after Dolly Madison's time, a democratic dish enjoyed by nearly all levels of society.

Dolly married James Madison in 1794 and became the White House hostess around 1801, when Thomas Jefferson entered it. The President, not having a wife of his own, borrowed Dolly to preside over meals. She served it at State dinners over which she presided both during Jefferson and her husband's administrations. A brilliant and innovative hostess, her often dramatic presentations of ice cream caught the public's fancy. Because of this historical association, Dolly Madison brand ice cream was created and named.

Venus Pen and Pencil Corp.

> *"It established the first factory for accurately graded*
> *leads in 17° (1905); developed the country's first*
> *line of thin lead coloring pencils (1920) and the first*
> *super thin black lead (1930)."*
>
> Accomplishments of
> Venus Pen and Pencil Co.

The Venus Pen and Pencil Corporation was formed in 1861 as the American Pencil Company, and three years later was renamed the American Lead Pencil Company. It was founded by Edward Weissenborn who migrated to the U.S. in 1854 after learning the pencil business from a Swiss manufacturer. In 1885, the firm was purchased by the Joseph Reckford Estate. It was incorporated in the same year with Louis J. Reckford, son of Joseph Reckford, as president.

The Venus tradename dates back to a trip Louis Reckford made to Paris in 1905, when he saw the Venus de Milo for the first time. The crackled finish trademark familiar to millions of American artists and engineers also came

Fig. 64. *"Venus" Pencils.* A Venus
pencil box showing both the Venus
de Milo trademark and the famous
crackled finish, which was originally achieved by accident.
Courtesy, *Faber-Castell*
Corporation

about with the manufacture of the first full line of American-made drawing
pencils, but by accident. Due to a defect, the green paint used on them
cracked when it dried. The officers of the company liked the effect so much
they had it simulated thereafter.

In 1956, the name of the American Lead Pencil Company was changed
to Venus Pen and Pencil Corporation because the Venus trademark had become so closely associated with Venus quality products.

159

10
MIS-NAMES AND FAILURES

"What would one expect of an "Edsel"? Something stodgy, unexciting? What might an "Edsel" be? Perhaps a pump or a circuit breaker."
"The Role of Design
Assessment in Product
Development" in *Package
Design* (1981)

There are many recorded instances of both mismarked names and poorly selected names. Some of these names fall into the exotic category while others have contributed toward the failure, in the marketplace, of the product. Why the name "peanut," when it is not truly a nut but rather a member of the legume family? Why did the now-bankrupt Sambo restaurant chain insist on keeping its racially insensitive name in the face of mounting consumer protest? And why does the West side Chinese restaurant in New York City, A Dish of Salt, keep its name when salt is associated with hypertension, heart disease and a host of other ills? On the other hand, Hardee's, the rapidly growing hamburger chain, has a name that does not go very well with a juicy piece of meat. They have counteracted this problem by introducing a new logotype. On their packaging, two concave, flowery-looking pieces of logotype form an H in a very soft fashion thus decreasing the hardness of the name itself.

MISMARKED PRODUCT NAMES

Foods appear to be one of major product categories that contain mismarked names. History and folklore have made these names both accepted and widely used.

1. *Wild rice* is really not rice, but the grain of an aquatic grass native to North America.

2. The *Muscovy duck* has nothing to do with Moscow. It was known simply as a musk duck, but somehow someone apparently presumed musk to be short for Muscovy and started calling it that by error.

3. The *Jerusalem artichoke* is actually a sunflower whose only possible connection to its geographical name may be the Italian word girasole, meaning "sunflower."

4. The recipe for *plum pudding* never includes plums.

5. The Chinese dish *shrimp in lobster sauce* never contains lobster.

6. Making Chinese *thousand-year-old eggs* actually takes about 100 days.

7. The *Jordan almond* does not come from the Kingdom of Jordan, but from Spain.

8. The *horse chestnut* is not eaten by either horses or people.

9. *Vaucluse asparagus* is an artichoke that grows wild in the Vaucluse region of France.

10. The *kiwi fruit* is not native to New Zealand and is really a Chinese gooseberry. It has nothing to do with the kiwi bird.

11. The origin of the name of the fish called *jewfish* is quite strange. It is a corruption of the Italian term "giupesce," which means bottom fish. It has nothing to do with the Jewish religion.

12. The meat dish called *London broil* is distinctly American and has absolutely nothing to do with England.

13. *Senegalese soup*, a curried cream-of-chicken soup, does not come from Senegal but from Ceylon.

PRODUCT FAILURES

Micrin Mouthwash

"When Johnson and Johnson brought the mouthwash Micrin to market in 1961, the company came on with all guns blazing. Within months, the new product had picked up 15 percent of the market and was threatening to overhaul that historical front-runner, the Warner-Lambert Company's Listerine."
N.Y. Times (Jan. 8, 1978)

Micrin mouthwash, introduced in 1961 and taken off the market in 1977, was a dismal failure in the marketplace. What went wrong? Johnson and Johnson seemed to have made all of the right marketing moves. Backed

161

by the alchemy of Louis Harris, the public opinion analyst, Micrin was colored blue—to differentiate it from the amber of Listerine, the red of Lavoris and the green of Green Mint.

Packaged in a sincere apothecary-type bottle and buttressed by a $15 million advertising campaign that focused on its "scientific" virtues, Micrin looked like a sure bet for the long haul. Instead, it turned out to be virtually a casebook study of what can go wrong with a product.

Micrin was regarded as somewhat dull and scientific with its name being no particular help. What would one expect of a product like Micrin? Certainly not a mouthwash but perhaps, something small. If the product had been in capsule form and dissolved in water, it would bear more relationship with its name.

In addition to Micrin's poor name, several other factors contributed to its failure. These included its color (there has never been a successful blue mouthwash), poor detailing and lack of promotion based on sex. Even when blue Micrin became green Micrin Plus, the "two-in-one mouthwash," it flopped after one year.

Edsel Automobile

By 1960, the name Edsel had become synonymous with "flop," "bomb" and "error." Why?

Introduced in September, 1957, its name was an initial source of problems. Ford Motor Company had originally asked the well-known American poet Marianne Moore to develop an engaging name for the new car. She and others suggested over 20,000 names including such names as: The Resilient Bullet, Pluma Piluma and Pastelogram. But over the objections of senior company management, the project directors selected the name Edsel. They felt it had "personal dignity and meaning to many of us." Many were the problems associated with the marketing of the car, but certainly the name itself did not aid in the acceptance of the product.*

The Edsel came to an end just two years and two months after it was first introduced. Ford had lost $250 million in invested capital, plus $200 million lost during production. Market analysts have selected four basic reasons for Edsel's failure (in addition to its name):

1. Between 1957–1960 medium-priced cars were declining in value in the marketplace. Sales had slid from 36.7 percent to 24.9 percent of the total

*In an association test conducted by Louis Cheskin in 1958, respondents were asked to associate the car image with one of the five years 1935, 1940, 1945, 1950, or 1955. The greatest number associated it with 1935. Hardly the youthful, futuristic appeal Edsel was aiming for!

car market. This change in car-buying patterns hurt Edsel.

2. Edsel styling, which had impressed so many viewers of its first model, had been modified in the interest of production economics.

3. Workmanship of the early production cars were sloppy.

4. The Edsel arrived just as the sudden recession of 1958 chopped the total car market down to nearly half of its former size.

Sinclair Oil

Sinclair Oil was a long established company that adopted a dinosaur symbol, disregarding the research information that the dinosaur was associated by consumers with "sluggish" and with other unfavorable terms, not with "power," "up-to-date," or "oil" as the chairman of the board thought. The name Sinclair is no longer in existence.

But if poorly selected names appear to contribute to the doom of a product, who can explain the success of:

1. *The J. M. Smucker Company*, which was described by Forbes magazine as "the General Motors of the jelly and jam business."

2. *Tabachnick's* (a rather hard to pronounce name), a firm that produces a line of frozen boil-in-bag soups.

3. *Manischewitz*, the famous kosher wine company.

4. *Volkswagen*, the name of a car developed by Hitler, but commonly used in Israel despite the still lingering animosity toward Germans. (Mercedes Benz is another example—little Mercedes was a favorite of Hitler and her father, Emile Jellinek, was an influential Nazi business leader. Mercedes gave her name to the product of the Daimler Company.)

The above examples illustrate that there is an exception to every rule. In the tricky business of selecting an effective brand name, there are really no hard and fast rules, only guidelines.

Because someone says that a particular market demands sober-sounding brand names does not mean that a whimsical name cannot win instant acceptance.

To know when to stay inside the boundaries of tradition and when to break from them, there must be a careful study of potential customers, the market and the competition.